Persia Portrayed

Envoys to the West, 1600-1842

D.T. Potts

MAGE PUBLISHERS

Mage Publishers Inc.
www.mage.com

Library of Congress Cataloging-in-Publication Data
Available at the Library of Congress

First hardcover edition
ISBN: 978-1949445-39-8

Visit Mage online: www.mage.com
Email: as@mage.com

CONTENTS

LIST OF FIGURES

Fig. 16. Sir William Beechey, Mirza Abu'l Hasan Khan (1776-1846), 1809-10. Oil on canvas. H: 56 8/10", W: 54 ¼". © Compton Verney, CVCSC:0358.B.—**31**

Fig. 17. Sir Thomas Lawrence, Mirza Abu'l Hassan Khan, 1810. Oil on canvas. H: 35", W: 27 ¼". Harvard Art Museums/Fogg Museum, Bequest of William M. Chadbourne, 1964.100.—**33**

Fig. 18. Moritz Michael Daffinger, Hussein Khan [Mirza 'Abdul Hoseyn Khan Shirazi]. Watercolor, gouache and graphite on paper, 1839. H: 6 ½", W: 5 1/8". Harry G. Sperling Fund, 2012, Metropolitan Museum of Art, 2012.471.—**36**

Fig. 19. Charles–Philibert de Lasteyrie, S. Ex. Mirza Aboul hassan Khan, Ambassadeur de Perse, 1819. Lithograph after a drawing by Eugène Delacroix. H: 13 3/10", W: 9 1/10". Inventaire du fonds français, graveurs du dix-neuvième siècle, Bibliothèque nationale, Département des estampes. Département Images et prestations numériques.—**41**

Fig. 20. Charles Motte, Aboul-Hassan, ambassadeur persan, 1819. Lithograph. H:?, W: ? Inventaire du fonds français, graveurs du dix-neuvième siècle, Bibliothèque nationale, Département des estampes. Département Images et prestations numériques.—**42**

Fig. 21. House of Gaetano Stefano Bartolozzi, Mirza Abul Hassan Envoy Extraordinary from the King of Persia, 1819. Lithograph after a drawing by The Honorable Miss E. H:?, W: ? Inventaire du fonds français, graveurs du dix-neuvième siècle, Bibliothèque nationale, Département des estampes. Département Images et prestations numériques.—**44**

Fig. 22. Maxim Gauci, His Excellency Mirza Abul Hassan Khan Ambassador Extraordinary, from his Majesty the Shah of Persia to H.R.H. the Prince Regent of Great Britain. To His Excellency Sir Gore Ouseley Bart., KLS KAS late Ambassador Extraordinary to the Court of Persia, this Lithographic Plate is respectfully dedicated (with permission) by his most humble Servant M. Gauci, 12 July 1819. Hand-colored lithograph. H: 14 6/10", W: 10 6/10". Victoria & Albert Museum, Purchased with the assistance of the National

Preface and Acknowledgments

This small book is a product of simple curiosity. It began with the portraits done in 1842 during the visit of Mar Yohanna, a bishop of the Assyrian Church of the East, to the United States. In seeking to put these in context, I began to examine portraits of other Persian notables done outside of Iran by Western artists and quickly realized that, as a group, these had never been the subject of a comprehensive study. Which Persians had their portraits done in Europe? Who were the artists? Who were the engravers? Despite considerable, ongoing interest in Qajar-era portraits by Iranian artists,[1] very few studies of any of the small number of portraits of notable Persians done in the West had been dealt with by art historians. For various reasons, mainly having to do with earlier work done on 18th and early 19th century Iranian history,[2] I have not expanded this survey beyond the reign of Mohammad Shah. In straightforward, practical terms, this can be justified by the great expansion in portraiture that followed the diffusion of the daguerreotype technique and the growth of diplomatic contacts, including royal visits, that characterized Iran in the latter half of the 19th century.

While I might be a scholar of Iran, particularly its archaeology and early history, I am certainly not an art historian by training. Hence the emphasis here is less on the sorts of issues that might seem most familiar to art historians, than on the history of the production of the work under discussion, and how it fits in with the missions undertaken by the individuals studied whose portraits have survived. Most of the work of discovery in the preparation of this study was done on my own, with an immense amount of help from the Google search engine. The scanning of literally millions of books and journals has made accessible

---

1. See the literature cited in n. 6 below.
2. Potts 2022, n.d.

sources of biographical information on both the artists and their subjects that would, in many cases, have remained hidden from view in pre-digitization times.

It is my privilege to illustrate several 'new' portraits here. I would particularly like to thank most warmly Mme Claude Sevaistre and her family for granting me permission to include an image of Louis-François Aubry's miniature portrait of 'Askar Khan-e Afshar Urumi (Fig. 10) in their family's collection, and Simon Ray (London) who generously allowed me to illustrate the pen and ink sketch of 'Askar Khan-e Afshar Urumi (Fig. 11) in his gallery. A number of other scholars kindly shared their expertise with me. For information on the Ukrainian-Russian painter Vladimir Lukich Borovikovsky, my sincerest thanks go to Polly Blakesley (Cambridge). For background on the Swiss artist Amélie Munier-Romilly, I would like to warmly thank Valérie Louzier-Gentaz (Geneva). For help with questions concerning Moritz Michael Daffinger, I would like to express my sincere appreciation to Nadine Orenstein (New York). For information on a portrait by Alexander Osipovitch Orlowski, exhibited in Philadelphia, I am grateful to Hoang Tran (Philadelphia). For answering questions on Gustav Adolph Hippius I would like to sincerely thank Firuza Melville (Cambridge). For help with sources on Georgian miniaturists I am indebted to Grigol Beradze (Tblisi). Finally, both Layla S. Diba (New York) and Willem Floor (Bethesda) answered questions on a number of occasions. Needless to say, any errors of fact or interpretation are my own responsibility.

The only point to note with respect to the bibliography is the fact that newspaper articles are cited only in the footnotes, not in the full bibliography, in order to avoid a tedious succession of 'Anonymous' entries from one and the same year in the case of multiple reports of Mar Yohanna's travels. In cases where a newspaper article is cited more than once, a complete citation will only be give for the first occurrence. Thereafter abbreviated references are used.

Finally, I would like to express my sincere thanks to my wife Hildy, a painter and sculptor herself, who never failed to raise important points during our many discussions of the artworks treated in this study.

THE PORTRAITS

In 1989 Ronald W. Ferrier asked three important questions: 'When…does the depiction of a *type* of personage in a Persian painting give way to the representation of a specific person? And to what extent has this ever been a Persian concern? Is the existence of a genre of Persian painted portraits, arguably beginning in the 10th/16th century, yet one more occurrence of foreign influences on the art of Persia from both East and West?'[3] Answers to all of these questions were offered over twenty years ago in Priscilla Soucek's wideranging study of theory and practice in Persianate portraiture. In addition to charting an increasing interest in portraiture during the Timurid period, Soucek noted the painter and poet Sadeqi Beg's belief that 'the outer form (*ṣūra*) of his portraits had almost been able to portray a person's *ma'nī* or inner essence,'[4] which brings to mind the Sanskrit concept *lakshana*, or those 'characteristic and cognitive attributes,' meant to imbue portraiture in Indian thought.[5] Persian portraiture, Soucek clearly demonstrated, was a reality with its own historical trajectory quite unrelated to contact with European tradition.

Between 1500, when the Safavid dynasty was founded, and 1848, when Naser al-Din Shah, Queen Victoria's contemporary, came to power, only a small number of Persian élites had their portraits painted. Within Iran portraiture was almost exclusively the province of court painters, many of whose names have survived,[6] effectively excluding all but persons of the highest rank from

---

3. Ferrier 1989: 223.

4. Soucek 2000: 106.

5. Ikeda 2019a: 21.

6. See e.g. Robinson 1963, 1986; Diba 1989; Diba and Ekhtiar; Floor 1999a: 125–154; Raby 2001; Rizvi 2012.

the institution of portraiture.[7] Ernst Gombrich's characterization of the portrait as a 'faithful construction of a relational model...constructed to any required degree of accuracy,' rather than 'a faithful record of a visual experience'[8] and Soucek's emphasis on the fact that all portraits are 'intrinsically idealized and... highly variable in their mode of execution'[9] are both helpful in assessing Persian portraiture and its diverse forms through time. It is also important to recognize, however, that portraits perform different functions depending on the context and the audience. Among other things, their purpose may be 'to support political power or to stress the social or economical status' of someone; to 'help to remember someone we lost;' or 'to help visualizing the face of people we never met,' as the Italian philosopher Paolo Spinicci has argued.[10] These functions may not necessarily be shared cross-culturally, however, and should not be assumed without evidence of their applicability in any given cultural context.

What then of portraits of Persians done outside of Iran? This is a topic that has received very little attention and constitutes the subject of the present study. Here the focus is on royal, diplomatic and other travellers on particular missions whose portraits were done in a variety of media in Europe and North America

---

7. On this point see the collection of miniature portraits of Persian élites in the Georgian National Museum in Koshoridze, Dgebuadze and Beradze 2013. The notion that only high-born individuals, or 'people of quality,' persons 'whose lives were...of interest to posterity,' were fitting subjects of portraits, the dissemination of which acted as 'a means... of encouraging the *popolo*'s obedience and respect,' is a view found commonly in Italian Renaissance treatises on art. See Woods-Marsden 2008: 362.

8. Gombrich 1969: 90.

9. Soucek 2000: 98.

10. Spinicci 2009: 43.

between the early 17[11] century and 1842.[11] Only about a dozen Iranians fall into this category, though several had their portraits done on multiple occasions. The sitters were almost all from the highest stratum of society, although several, who participated in an 1829 diplomatic mission to St. Petersburg, while educated, were decidedly inferior, socially speaking, to the royalty they accompanied, and one, a Christian priest from Gol'adhan, near Salmas, who visited the United States in 1842 in company with the American missionary, Justin Perkins, was from a humble background. This, however, was no longer an impediment to having one's portrait painted.[12]

SHAH 'ABBAS I'S AMBASSADORS

Until the late 18th century, very few portraits of Persian done in the West can be cited. However, three of the earliest portraits of Persians done outside the country date to the first years of the 17th century. These were the work of the gifted Netherlandish artist Aegidius Sadeler II (1568–1629) who was summoned to Prague in 1597 by the Holy Roman Emperor, Rudolf II (r. 1576–1612) and became his imperial engraver.[13] It was in this capacity that Sadeler engraved the portraits of three different Persian ambassadors — Hoseyn 'Ali Beg (Fig.

---

11. One well-known subject who falls outside the scope of this study by virtue of her Circassian origin is the wife of Sir Anthony Shirley, Teresa Sampsonia, on whom see Schwartz 2013: 86-87, and Andrea 2017: 124-130. In 1622 Sir Anthony Van Dyck painted her portrait in oils in Rome. It is now in the Petworth House and Park collection; see https://www.nationaltrustcollections.org.uk/object/486170. At least two other oil portraits of her are known, one by Sir Thomas B. Western in Anonymous 1866a: 69, and another by William Larkin (previously attributed to Marcus Geeraerts the Younger, owned by the National Trust for Scotland, for which see https://www.vads.ac.uk/digital/collection/ NIRP/id/28138/. Goetz 1938: 287 singled out Lady Shirley as the only Persian [sic] woman to have had her portrait painted in the 17th century. Van Dyck did a sketch of her as well that survives in one of his sketch books in the British Museum; see https://www. britishmuseum.org/collection/object/P_1957-1214-207-60. Miniatures of Lady Shirley are also known. See e.g. one attributed to Nicholas Hilliard and two attributed to Isaac Oliver in Holme and Kennedy 1917: 30, 32.

12. Already in 1545 Pietro Aretino (1492-1556) wrote, 'It's your shame, oh century, to tolerate that tailors and butchers appear living in portraits.' See Woods-Marsden 2008: 362. Similarly, in 1796 the Earl of Fife said, incorrectly to judge from Aretino's remark, that 'before this century, very few people presented themselves to a painter, except those who were of great families or remarkable for their actions in the service of their country,' whereas, in his day, 'every body almost who can afford twenty pounds has portraits of himself, wife, and children painted.' Quoted in Elliott 2012: 81.

13. Limouze 1989: 7.

Fig. 1. Hoseyn 'Ali Beg, Shah 'Abbas I's ambassador to the Holy Roman Emperor, Rufolf II, was memorialized by the Emperor's imperial engraver, Aegidius Sadeler II. The Persian envoy travelled in company with Sir Anthony Shirley who, together with his brother Robert, had visited the court of Shah 'Abbas I in 1598. Unlike the portraits of the other two Persian ambassadors who followed him (Figs. 2-3), this one focuses less on the textiles worn than on the fur-lined coat which, given that Hoseyn 'Ali Beg was sent on his mission in January, would have been an essential part of his dress.

1), Zeynal Khan (Fig. 2) and Mehdi Qoli Beg (Fig. 3) — all of whom were sent by Shah 'Abbas I (r. 1588–1629), the Safavid ruler of Persia, in 1601, 1604 and 1604/5, respectively, to negotiate an anti-Ottoman alliance between Persia and the Holy Roman Empire.[14] The French miniaturist Esaye Le Gillon (fl. 1590–1610), likewise employed at Rudol's court,[15] also painted miniatures of both Mehdi Qoli Beg and Zeynal Khan.[16] As Waldemar Deluga observed, 'The Persians must have excited as much curiosity in Kraków as the Muscovite legation, mainly because of their exotic character, especially their dress and horse trappings, which were totally unlike anything yet seen within the borders of the Polish Lithuanian Commonwealth.'[17]

Mohammad Reza Beg, Shah Soltan Hoseyn's ambassador to Louis XIV

In 1715 Mohammad Reza Beg arrived in Paris and, like many diplomatic visitors from distant lands, became a personnage of fascination for the French public.[18] A miniature by Antoine Coypel (1661-1722), sold by Sotheby's in 2007, appears to be an unvarnished likeness.[19] A seated drawing of a Persian by Antoine Watteau (1684-1721), often considered a portrait of the ambassador, is

---

14. Deluga 2008: 424.

15. See in general Kaufmann 1988. As Boon 1992: 300 noted, Le Gillon was 'an artist at the Imperial Court at Prague, about whom we know virtually nothing.' It is certain, however, that he was the nephew of the botanist and polymath Charles de l'Écluse, or Carolus Clusius (1526–1609), and it has been suggested that he was the artist responsible for eighty-seven watercolors of Pannonian mushrooms, the so-called Codex Clusii. See Schaechter 1997: 9–10. The illustrations were actually paid for by the Hungarian magnate Balthasar (III) Batthyány (Boldiszar de Batthyani) who hosted Clusius at his castle in Nemet-Ujvar (mod. Güssing, Austria), and was employed as a bailiff in the court in Vienna. See Wille 2001: 88.

16. The latter is now in the Qatar Museum of Islamic Art. See https://www.qm.org.qa/en/portrait-of-sinal-shah-kamlu.

17. Deluga 2008: 426. The significance of dress, headgear and other accoutrements to Late Renaissance viewers of portraits like these should not be underestimated. As Howarth 1997: 107 noted, in discussing Tudor portraiture, 'An Elizabethan portrait depends for its effect on "reading" the emblems in jewels, clothes, animals, furniture, or objects held in the hand. It is a biography not merely a likeness.'

18. For overviews of the embassy see Herbette 1907; Castellucio 2006: 37-44; Mokhberi 2020: 86-111.

19. Coypel was also responsible for a large oil painting showing the ambassador's audience with Louis XIV in the Château de Versailles.

Fig. 2. Zeynal Khan Shamlu's embassy to Prague was undoubtedly one of the highlights of his life, though he came away from it convinced that his European host had no intention of aiding his master. As Father John Thaddeus, a Carmelite father in Isfahan, wrote to a colleague on May 14th, 1609, Zeynal Khan 'had written ill of the Emperor and the Christian princes, saying that all their professions of friendship were false, and that all they wanted was for the Turks and Persians to destroy each other and the Muslim religion included.'

Fig. 3. Aegidius Sadeler II's portrait of Mehdi Qoli Beg shows the Persian envoy wearing costly silk garments. Such fine materials were probably familiar to the artist for Sadeler was a native of Antwerp which, in the late 16th century, was one of the principal markets for Persian silk, much of it coming from Venetian merchants who controlled the westward flow of this precious commodity through Damascus and Aleppo.

Fig. 4. Mohammad Reza Beg and his entourage arrived in Paris on February 7th, 1715, and four days later were received by Louis XIV at Versailles. The Persian envoy had his audience of leave on August 13th. This proved to be the last official duty performed by Louis XIV who died on September 1st. While in France, a host of images of Mohammad Reza Beg circulated, one of which even showed him in the bath.

Fig. 5. This equestrian portrait of Mohammad Reza Beg has many points in common with contemporary depictions of European monarchs, including the Persian envoy's host, Louis XIV, on rearing chargers. Such images presented their subjects as powerful, victorious, militaristic sovereigns. Mohammad Reza Beg wears the same elaborate tunic seen in Fig. 4, while his horse is covered with an exquisite saddle blanket. The envoy's stirrup resembles 18th century damascened iron examples from the Ottoman empire.

Fig. 6. Aga Mohammad Shah's brother, Morteza Qoli Khan, fled to Russian territory after the accession of his brother. The Qajar shah's invasion of the Caucasus prompted Catherine II to order Valerian Zubov to push the Persian forces back, depose Aga Mohammad and install Morteza Qoli Khan on the Qajar throne. Although Catherine II kept the Persian exile at arm's length, refusing to let him come to St. Petersburg, the Borovikovsky portraits show that he eventually travelled to the capital.

probably not.[20] The individual is beardless, whereas the stylized engravings of 'Mehemet Reza Beg' always depict him with a beard. Engravings of a seated portrait of the ambassador, as well as an equestrian portrait, were published at the time of his visit (Figs. 4-5).

MORTEZA QOLI KHAN

Following these portraits there seems to have been a long hiatus during which no further portraits of Persian notables done in the West are recorded. The story of Western portraiture of Persians resumes again in 1796 with a life-size portrait of Morteza Qoli Khan (Fig. 6), brother of Aga Mohammad Shah (r. 1789–1797), the founder of the Qajar dynasty, painted in St. Petersburg by the Ukrainian-Russian painter, Vladimir Lukich Borovikovsky (1757-1825). At this time Borovikovsky, the 'Russian Gainsborough,'[21] was the leading portraitist at the court of Catherine II (the Great).[22] Morteza Qoli Khan was a political refugee who had fled to Russia a decade earlier in an effort to escape his murderous brother,[23] Aga Mohammad Shah. The founder of the Qajar Dynasty was not unique among Iranian rulers and aspirants to the throne in considering it imperative that all potential rivals, whether siblings, cousins or those unrelated by blood, be eliminated. This most often took the form of capture and execution, although occasionally a measure of clemency was exercised and rivals were merely blinded before being sent into internal exile.[24] Thus, when Morteza Qoli Khan took refuge in Russia, his behavior was eminently rational. In 1787, according to Muriel Atkin, when Russia failed to reach a trade accord with Aga Mohammad Khan, before he

---

20. It is entitled by the Louvre simply 'Persan assis,' even though a handwritten note on the reverse of the drawing identifies it as the Persian ambassador. See https://collections.louvre.fr/en/ark:/53355/cl020038609.

21. Hare 1965: 119. Borovikovsky has also been termed an unrivaled master of 'virtuoso technique, the idealization of subject, [and] the ceremonial format,' who 'drew freely from European classical models.' See Stites 2005: 305.

22. For his career see e.g. Leek 1999: 49.

23. Olivier 1808: 181-182.

24. This was the case with Khosrow Mirza and Jahangir Mirza, two brothers of Mohammad Shah (r. 1834–1848) whom he blinded. As a contemporary observer noted, 'Mohammed Shah was seized with some foolish and unjust ideas. It entered into his mind that they were beloved by the Azerbajan people, and he thought that they might do some mischief. This idea being continually present to his mind, he…had these two brothers brought before him, and ordered their eyes to be put out. This was done immediately, and those unfortunate young Princes lost their eyes; moreover, they were imprisoned in the castle of Ardabil.' See Kayat 1839: 14-15.

became Shah, Catherine II determined to depose Aga Mohammad Khan and install Morteza Qoli Khan as her vassal. Although Catherine forbade him from coming to St.Petersburg, so as to have him at the ready in southeastern Russia when the time was right to overthrow his brother,[25] the Borovikovsky portrait clearly proves that Morteza Qoli Khan did in fact succeed in making his way to St. Petersburg. Moreover, Catherine herself commissioned the work. A smaller version of the portrait, showing Morteza Qoli Khan in a similar stance but wearing a much darker gown, and with landscape in the background, minus the human figures seen in the larger version, is in the Tretyakov Gallery (Fig. 7). Given the fact that Catherine II commissioned Morteza Qoli Khan's portrait, it would be logical to assume that the larger one was the 'official' portrait. It is not known just why the smaller version was painted, but perhaps it was meant for Morteza Qoli Khan to keep himself.[26]

Several details about Morteza Qoli Khan stand out. With regard to his stance, Rosalind P. Blakesley has stressed that 'Borovikovsky deployed a pose common in full-length state portraits, and a low viewpoint to emphasize his subject's regal presence.' Moreover, there is an obvious emphasis on 'the finer points of weaponry and trim' which 'accentuates the prince's alterity, much as exotic difference was highlighted in other 'oriental' portraits of the time.'[27] Morteza Qoli Khan's posture, while not necessarily suggesting that he had delusions of grandeur, clearly indicates his pretensions to the highest position in his country, pretensions that were sustained by no less a figure than Catherine, Empress of all the Russias. As for his accoutrements, even the most cursory perusal of literature on élite Qajar Persian dress makes it abundantly clear that members of the élite revelled in their costly garments and jewels. It is scarcely surprising, therefore, to find that a string of pearl worry beads is suspended from the right hand of Morteza Qoli Khan, and each of his pinky fingers is adorned with a precious ring. Moreover, his ceremonial sword with sapphire-encrusted hilt, like his bejwelled

---

25. Atkin 1980: 35, 63.

26. My sincere thanks to Polly Blakesley, Pembroke College, University of Cambridge, for sharing her thoughts on this intriguing pair of portraits. As she has pointed out (pers. comm.), the two portraits could have been made to hang in different venues, in order to spread the news of Catherine II's largesse and magnanimity towards the Persian exile. In this case, however, the smaller portrait is not a copy of the larger one, as differences in dress and background make clear.

27. Blakesley 2010: 826.

Fig. 7. Because of Morteza Qoli Khan's dark garment, many details of his accoutrements are clearer than in the larger version of his portrait (Fig. 6). The bejwelled hilt of his dagger; the colors of his kamarband; the individual beads of his rosary (tasbih); the pinky rings on each hand; and even the henna on his fingernails, are all perfectly visible. Morteza Qoli Khan's beard is also visibly shorter than in the larger portrait (Fig. 6), the turbaned attendants of which have been replaced by an idealized landscape.

sword belt, tassel and dagger, clearly ooze wealth, as does his lambskin cloak with heavy embroidered backing, and the elaborate Cashmere shawl wrapped around his head. He was, after all, a Qajar prince.

'ABBAS MIRZA

As things turned out, Aga Mohammad Shah was not deposed in favor of his brother Morteza Qoli Khan, but rather was assassinated in 1797, in an event unrelated to Russian intrigue, roughly a year after his brother's portrait was painted. Aga Mohammad Shah was succeeded by his favorite nephew Baba Khan, better known outside the Qajar royal family as Fath 'Ali Shah who, faced with Russian expansion in the Caucasus, and disappointed by what he considered Britain's lukewarm support of his own aspirations, desperately sought an alliance with Napoleon. In 1807, as a result of the Franco-Persian treaty signed at Fincken-stein on 4 May of that year, Napoleon sent an embassy to Fath 'Ali Shah under General Claude-Matthieu Gardane (1766–1818) which included a number of young French military officers who were meant to train different branches of the Persian armed forces.[28] One of these was the Swiss-born military engineer Auguste de Bontems (1782–1854). A graduate of the École Polytechnique in Paris, Bontems had been with Napoleon's Grand Army since 1805. In Iran he was engaged in drafting plans for fortifications, spending most of his time working directly for the Qajar crown prince, 'Abbas Mirza, and teaching a select few of his officers the rudiments of geometry, algebra, engineering, architectural drafting and the theory of fortifications.

Just a few years earlier the French diplomat and Orientalist, Pierre Amédée Jaubert (1779–1847), had been sent on a diplomatic mission to Fath 'Ali Shah, from which he returned in 1806. Although it was not until 1821 that Jaubert published an account of his travels, that volume contained, as its frontispiece, a lithographic portrait of 'Abbas Mirza (Fig. 8), based on a sketch made by Bontems while he was working for 'Abbas Mirza which, according to its legend, was drawn in Geneva by 'Mademoiselle de Romilly.'[29] This was none other than the Swiss portraitist Jeanne Louise Amélie Romilly (1788–1875) or Munier-Romilly after her marriage in 1821 to David Munier,[30] a student of one of her father's friends, the painter Firmin Massot (1766-1849). Denied access to the great

---

28. Potts in press.

29. 'Dessiné à Genève, par Mlle de Romilly d'après un tableau original communiqué par le Lieutenant A. de Bontems.' See Jaubert 1821: unpaginated frontispiece.

30. For her life see Chenevière 1916, a biography written by her grandson.

Fig. 8. While serving as a member of General Gardane's mission to the court of Fath 'Ali Shah, Auguste de Bontems sketched a portrait of 'Abbas Mirza that was later turned into a proper, painted miniature by the Swiss artist Amélie Romilly-Munier. Whether the original, on which this lithograph was based, still survives is unknown. Born in 1789, 'Abbas Mirza would have been about 18 or 19 years old when Bontems captured his likeness.

schools of fine arts and the academy,[31] Munier-Romilly nevertheless excelled at portraiture, like her teacher Massot, and is said to have painted over 5000 portraits during her career, ranging from early works using a Conté crayon and stump, to later ones in oil or pastels.[32] It is impossible to say just when Bontems' sketch of 'Abbas Mirza was transformed into a full-fledged portrait. Bontems returned to Geneva from Gardane's mission in 1808, but as Jaubert's book was not published until 1821, it could have been done anytime between 1808 and 1821 when the portrait of 'Abbas Mirza was published and Mademoiselle de Romilly, its creator, married David Munier, becoming Madame Munier-Romilly.[33] How it came about that Bontems sought out Amélie Romilly is unknown. As both were from Genevan families it is probable that they were acquainted with each other, or perhaps it was simply Romilly's growing reputation as a society portraitist that led Bontems to approach her. Alternatively, if Bontems knew Firmin Massot, the teacher may have recommended his pupil Romilly for the task of converting Bontems sketch into a finished portrait.

'ASKAR KHAN AFSHAR URUMI

A second lithographic portrait included in Jaubert's volume depicts 'Askar Khan Afshar Urumi (Fig. 9), who was sent by Fath 'Ali Shah to Paris as his ambassador to Napoleon,[34] and whom Bontems accompanied when he returned from Iran to Paris.[35] A minuscule inscription beneath the portrait in Jaubert's volume states that the original on which the lithograph was based was 'painted from life by Aubry.'[36] This laconic reference identifies the artist as the renowned French miniaturist Louis-François Aubry (1767–1851) who certainly never visited Iran and hence must have painted 'Askar Khan's portrait when the ambassador was in

---

31. More specifically, Munier-Romilly lamented her inability to have an opportunity to draw nude models, for she was obliged to draw only clothed ones. As she noted, 'Le corps nu a été l'obstacle décisif pour les femmes artistes qui n'avaient pas accès aux écoles des beaux-arts ni aux études d'académie. Le portrait inévitablement leur seul apanage artistique.' See Lorenz 2010: 59-60.

32. Veillon 1908.

33. Lorenz 2010: 60.

34. Busse 1972: 122.

35. 'Askar Khan arrived in Paris on 19 July, 1808, and was installed in the former residence of Mlle de Conti in [12] rue de Fréjus, since renamed rue Monsieur in the 7e arrondissement. See Simond 1900: 175.

36. 'Peint d'après nature par Aubry.' Legend at the bottom of the portrait inserted between pages 254 and 255 in Jaubert 1821.

Fig. 9. At least five portraits of 'Askar Khan Afshar Urumi survive from his two year-long visit to Paris (1808-1810). This lithograph was done from a miniature (Fig. 10) by the master portraitist, Louis-François Aubry. Buried in Amédée Jaubert's *Voyage en Arménie et en Perse* (1821), it was nevertheless labelled, in a minuscule legend, as having been based on an original by Aubry.

Paris. After entering the Académie Royale de Peinture et de Sculpture in 1784, Aubry studied with Louis Jean-Jacques Durameau (1733–96), François-André Vincent (1746–1816) and Jean-Baptiste Isabey (1767–1855).[37] Only seven years later, in 1791, he was made a Membre de l'Académie and in 1793 had his first exhibition in Paris. Besides being a formidable technician whose coloration and rendering of costume and background were unequalled, Aubry was also a teacher who produced numerous highly successful pupils.[38] His biogaphical entry in Nagler's lexicon, published in 1835 while Aubry was still alive, noted that his output after 1801 was prodigious, and that many of his miniatures and drawings were in galleries in France and elsewhere in Europe. Nor was his output confined to miniatures. He was responsible for two much lauded, full-length portraits (c. 1808), now at Fontainebleau, of the King (Jérôme Bonaparte) and Queen (Catherine of Wurtemberg) of Westphalia.[39] According to Leo Schidlof, Aubry surpassed his teacher Isabey but, because he devoted so much time to the training of his pupils, he produced fewer miniatures than might have been expected, relatively few of which have survived.[40] Aubry's portrait of 'Askar Khan (Fig. 10) is currently in the Sevaistre family, one of whose ancestors was married to Jaubert.[41] Studies of European miniatures and of Aubry's output in particular have, unsurprisingly, failed to notice the minute inscription below 'Askar Khan's portrait in Jaubert's volume attributing it to the French master, nor do any of the anecdotal accounts that survive about 'Askar Khan's time in Paris mention him having his portrait painted by Aubry.

The lithographs of the portraits of both 'Abbas Mirza and 'Askar Khan in Jaubert's *Voyage en Arménie et en Perse* were executed by the German-Danish lithographer Wilhelm (Vilhelm) Heuer (1788–1856).[42] Born in Ludwigslust in the

---

37. On Isabey as a teacher, and the convention of pupils acknowledging this as a badge of honor, see Lécosse 2013: 103. From 1800 onwards Aubry styled himself pupil of 'Citizens Vincent and Isabey.' See Lécosse 2013: 111, n. 53.

38. Aronson and Wieseman 2006: 89.

39. Nagler 1835: 184.

40. Schidlof 1964: 14. For six examples of his work in the Tansey Miniatures Foundation (Celle, Germany) see https://tansey-miniatures.com/en/collection.

41. Sevaistre 1996: 191, 'Je possède une miniature d'Aubry représentant un barbu coiffé d'un turban gigantsque: c'est Asker Khan, ambassadeur de Perse à Paris de 1808 à 1810.' Jaubert's sister Angélique (1785–1843) married the Sevaistres' ancestor, Georges Outrey, one of several Outreys who served as French diplomats, principally in the Ottoman empire.

42. Not to be confused with the better known graphic artist Christian Ludwig Wilhelm Heuer (1813-1890), also known as Wilhelm, from Hamburg, for whose work see Salamon 1996. He does not seem to have been a relation of the elder Wilhelm (Vilhelm) Heuer.

Fig. 10. Set in a small gilded frame, Aubry's miniature portrait of 'Askar Khan Afshar Urumi is a tiny masterpiece. From the extraordinarily lifelike rendering of the folds in the Persian ambassador's turban, to the skin tones and shadows of his brow and nose, his piercing eyes, the hair of his beard, and the hilt of the dagger just visible against his patterned red dress, Aubry has crafted an image that is as replete with significant detail as it is arresting. It is published here for the first time.

Duchy of Mecklenburg-Schwerin, Heuer entered the Royal Danish Academy of Fine Arts (Kunstakademiet) in Copenhagen in 1803 where he won several gold and silver medals for his copper plate etchings. He became a naturalized Danish citizen in 1816 and in 1818 was given a travel stipend to visit Paris. In November, 1820, he applied for an extension of his stipend but was granted only a portion of what he required. Nevertheless, he seems to have remained in Paris until 1823, returning to Denmark the following year. In 1830 he submitted an etching of a portrait of the Danish sculptor Albert Bertel Thorvaldsen (1770-1844), by Christoffer Wilhelm Eckersberg (1783-1853), to the Danish Academy, seeking membership, but was unsuccessful.[43] After his Paris sojourn, at which time he presumably did the etchings of the ʿAskar Khan and ʿAbbas Mirza portraits for Jaubert's book, Heuer lived most of his life in Hamburg and Copenhagen, only rarely exhibiting his work.[44]

ʿAskar Khan is known to have thrown himself into Parisian life while he was there,[45] and it is therefore not surprising that at least three other portraits were done of him. Anne-Louis Girodet de Roucy-Trioson (1767-1824), considered one of Jacques-Louis David's most celebrated pupils,[46] is thought to have been the creator of a pastel portrait[47] (Fig. 11) donated to the Louvre in 1879 by the draftsman and painter Pierre François Lehoux (1803-1892), a student of Horace Vernet (1789-1863). A pen and ink sketch (Fig. 12) of ʿAskar Khan's head and

---

43. Weilbach 1877-1878: 279. Eckersberg executed three portraits of Thorvaldsen, the first when the two artists shared lodgings in Rome in 1814. Eckersberg sent this painting, entitled *Portrait of Bertel Thorvaldsen wearing the gown of the Accademia di San Luca in front of his frieze showing Alexander's Entry into Babylon*, an oil on canvas (H: 35 8/10", W: 29 1/10"), to the Royal Danish Academy of Fine Arts as a gift. He also painted two later versions, in 1832 and 1838. The final version is in the Ny Carlsberg Glyptotek (Copenhagen). See Oliver 2006: 52.

44. Weilbach 1877-1878: 279-280 gives a full account of Heuer's career. See also Müller and Singer 1896: 173.

45. For a series of amusing anecdotes derived from ʿAskar Khan's stay in Paris, from the perspective of Napoleon's valet, see Wairy 1830: 49–57. A more serious view is given in Amini 1999: 140–6.

46. See e.g. the extensive biography in Coupin de la Couperie 1829: i–liii; Delécluze 1860: 254–273.

47. Cabinet des dessins, Fonds des dessins et miniatures, Département des arts graphiques, Musée du Louvre. H: 11.8"; W. 9.1". http://arts-graphiques.louvre.fr/detail/oeuvres/1/112449-Portrait-dAsker-Khan The attribution rests on the fact that the backing of the drawing was labelled "Girodet." Thus, the 1911 catalogue of drawings in the Louvre notes, 'sur le montage: Girodet. Donné par M. Lehoux, en septembre 1879.' See Anonymous 1911: 15.

ASKER-KAN

AMBASSADEUR DE PERSE
A PARIS

Fig. 11. This portrait in profile, which may be the work of Girodet, conveys the mass and volume of the ambassador's high turban and rounded shoulders, beneath a fur-trimmed, outer cloak. The scabbard and hilt of the dagger, encrusted with pearls, turquoise and rubies (?), complement the rich, patterned textiles in which the envoy is clothed. The serious countenance, highlit brow and crows feet reflect both the 'Askar Khan Afshar Urumi's dignity and his age.

shoulders, in profile, shows the Persian envoy in a posture remarkably close to that seen in Girodet's portrait. It bears a label written along the lefthand side of the paper, 'Croquis d'Asker Kan ambassadeur du roi de Perse en 1808 par David.' While David is not known to have executed a finished portrait of 'Askar Khan, the similarity of the sketch to Girodet's work, and the fact that Girodet and David were extremely close,[48] raises the possibility that David gave his sketch of 'Askar Khan to his pupil Girodet, who then annotated it with the handwritten label.[49] This possibility is reinforced, if not absolutely confirmed, by the handwriting on the sketch which closely resembles that of a letter written by Girodet on 16 April, 1802, to his friend Ange-René Ravault (1766-1845).[50]

A portrait of 'Askar Khan in oils on canvas by Joseph Franque (1774–1833), entitled 'S[on]. Exc[ellence]. Asker-Khan, ambassadeur de Perse,' painted in 1810,[51] is today in the Pushkin Museum, Moscow (Fig. 13). Like Girodet, Franque was also a student of David's but by 1814 he had emigrated to Italy where, through the good offices of Elisa Bonaparte, Grand Duchess of Tuscany, he obtained the offer of a post as professor of drawing in Carrara. Unable to take up the position because of the political situation in the country, Franque moved to Naples where he became an honorary professor at the Accademia di Belle Arti in 1822. In 1823 his 'Scene during the Eruption of Vesuvius,' now in the Philadelphia Museum of Art,[52] won first prize in a competition and he was named professor of painting. Although his date of death is usually given as 1833, Franque was still active at Naples in 1839.[53]

Perhaps the most well-known Parisian portrait of 'Askar Khan, however, is that of Césarine Henriette Flore Davin-Mirvault (1773–1844), yet another pupil of David's who also studied with his arch rival, Joseph-Benoit Suvée (1743-1807), and with the renowned miniaturist Jean-Baptiste Jacques Augustin (1759-1832).

48. This is very clear from the many anecdotes of Girodet's life which illustrate his life-long relationship with David. See Delécluze 1860: 254–273. In a letter to Isabey, David acknowledged Girodet as one of the students whose work did him the greatest honor ('les élèves qui m'ont le plus fait honneur'). See Dagorne 2005: 12.

49. My sincere thanks to Simon M.W. Ray of Simon Ray Limited, Indian & Islamic Works of Art, London, for information on the David drawing and for permission to illustrate it here.

50. The letter belongs to the Site des Archives historiques et généalogiques, Orléans, France. For a facsimile see https://archives-loiret.fr/vie-culturelle-2/documents-du-mois/250e-anniversaire-de-la-naissance-du-peintre-montargois-anne-louis-girodet-trioson.

51. Kuznetsova 1980: 379, no. 209.

52. Rosenthal 1979: 6.

53. Brun-Durand 1900: 340.

Fig. 12. This quickly drawn profile sketch of 'Askar Khan Afshar Urumi, by Jacques-Louis David, is published here for the first time. The view, in profile, shows an obvious similarity to the portrait attributed to Girodet (Fig. 11), and the handwriting closely resembles Girodet's as well. Whether David, who was Girodet's teacher, made this sketch during the same sitting in which the portrait thought to have been done by Girodet was done, is unknown, but certainly a possibility.

Fig. 13. Joseph Franque's portrait of 'Askar Khan Afshar Urumi shows him wearing much costlier garments than those seen in Figs. 9-12. It is a portrait of contrasts: the golden turban against the sky; the deep black beard against the ambassador's golden dress; the red kamarband and the white fur lining of his heavy cloak, are all striking. 'Askar Khan's facial features are enveloped in his dark hair, shown protruding from his golden turban, and full beard. His gaze off into the distance is almost ominous.

Fig. 14. Davin-Mirvault's portrait of a kneeling 'Askar Khan Afshar Urumi accentuates the richness of the textiles displayed: the sumptuous golden garment, with its blue trim emerging under the cuffs; the striped red and white kamarband; the light-colored turban with bands of decoration; the brown fur lining of the pale red cloak; and the patterning of the carpet. The extreme length of the pipe stem in 'Askar Khan's right hand, capped by what appears to be an ivory mouthpiece, is striking.

Exhibited at the Salon in 1810, Davin-Mirvault's portrait of 'Askar Khan (Fig. 14) was acquired by King Louis-Philippe I of France for the palace at Versailles.[54] Davin-Mirvault also exhibted a second portrait of 'Askar Khan at the Salon of 1814.[55] Discussing Davin-Mirvault's work as a miniaturist, Henri Bouchot noted that she was, from the outset, a married woman who needed to work to survive and was looking to acquire a marketable skill. Thus, she was interested less in perfecting the art of miniature painting than she was in the acquisition of the mechanics of teaching.[56] Her school of painting and drawing for young women, which had opened by 1805, only closed with her death in 1844.[57]

Davin-Mirvault's portrait is striking in many ways. From the masterfully executed turban, to the gold, patterned garment, the fur-lined cape, the pattern and blue trim of the lining of 'Askar Khan's gown, the string of pearl worry beads, or the hennaed fingernails, it is an utterly arresting image of 'Oriental' luxury, a proxy for the pretensions of Fath 'Ali Shah vis-à-vis the all-powerful Napoleon. Whatever criticisms Henri Bouchot may have levelled at the artist, Davin-Mirvault certainly succeeded in rendering 'Askar Khan's facial features and beard with fastidious, compelling confidence. Surely this is the image of an imperial envoy on a mission.

The last portrait produced during 'Askar Khan's stay in Paris appears on a large bronze medallion, 14 4/10" in diameter, on which the ambassador is depicted in profile. Sold at auction in 2012,[58] it is today in the private collection of Count Charles-André Colonna Walewski, a direct descendant of Napoleon. The medallion bears an inscription running around almost the entire circumference of the piece, which reads: 'ASKER KHAN AMBASSADEUR EXTRAORDINAIRE DE S M L EMPEREUR DE PERSE PRES LA COUR IMPERIALE DE FRANCE.'[59] There is no indication of who was responsible for casting this medallion.[60] In addition to 'Askar Khan's

---

54. Fine 1983: 19; Arasa 2019: 21.

55. See Anonymous 1814: 24. Cf. Bellier de la Chavignerie and Auvray 1882: 362, s.v. Davin (Mme Césarine-Henriette-Flore, née Mirvault).

56. Bouchot 1910: 234, 'Ce qu'elle demande à Augustin, c'est bien moins un perfectionnement dans l'art de miniature, qu'une gymnastique d'enseignement.' Cf. Halliday 1999: 192.

57. Anonymous 1805: 128; Bouchot 1910: 235. Cf. Bellier de la Chavignerie and Auvray 1882: 362.

58. Beaussant and Lefèvre 2012: 43, lot 170.

59. See https://colonnawalewski.ch/9i257/#.

60. The medallion is not mentioned in e.g. Mercey 1852: 401–433; Marx 1897; or Rondot 1904.

sumptuous beard, his tightly wound turban draws the eye, particularly as it occupies roughly half of the area of the portrait bust.

MIRZA 'ABU'L HASAN KHAN SHIRAZI

Unfortunately for Fath 'Ali Shah, the anticipated Franco-Persian alliance so longed for failed to materialize, largely because the Treaty of Tilsit, signed on 7 July, 1807, which briefly made Russia and France allies, put an immediate stop to Napoleon's plan to support Fath 'Ali Shah's territorial claims in the Caucasus and his war effort against Russia. With that, Britain was able to once more gain the upper hand in the Anglo-French tug-of-war for Fath 'Ali Shah's loyalty and to supplant the French. In 1809 Sir Harford Jones negotiated a treaty with the Court of Tehran, after which Fath 'Ali Shah dispatched Mirza 'Abu'l Hasan Khan Shirazi (1776–1845) to London where he waited almost eight months for the British government to ratify the accord. The Persian ambassador arrived at Portsmouth on 29 November, 1809, and left from the same port on 18 July, 1810.[61] During his stay, Mirza 'Abu'l Hasan Khan Shirazi's portrait was painted by Sir William Beechey (1753-1839) (twice), Lady Anne Beechey (1764-1833) and Sir Thomas Lawrence (1769-1830), while two portrait busts were done by the sculptor John Bacon, Jr. (1777-1859). Thanks primarily to dated entries in the published diary of Mirza 'Abu'l Hasan Khan Shirazi it is possible to assess these works in chronological order.

Mirza 'Abu'l Hasan Khan Shirazi's diary entry for Monday, 29 January, 1810, reads, 'I went with Sir Gore Ouseley and Mr. Morier[62] to the house of Sir William Beechey,[63] the portrait painter who lives near the church and my house. Sir Gore Ouseley told me that the East India Company had asked him to arrange for a likeness of me to be made and for this reason he troubled me to accompany him to the artist's studio....Sir William Beechey asked me to be

---

61. Cloake 1988: 9. For a reconstruction of the entire chronology and itinerary of Mirza 'Abu'l Hasan Khan Shirazi's mission, see Vahdat 2017: Appendix A (unpaginated).

62. James Justinian Morier (1780–1849) had been a member of Sir Harford Jones' embassy, and accompanied Mirza 'Abu'l Hasan Khan Shirazi on his journey to England. He also continued to act as an aide to Sir Gore Ouseley in London and returned to Iran with Sir Gore and Mirza 'Abu'l Hasan Khan. For his life see Johnston 1998. For Morier's own account of his journey to England see Morier 1812.

63. At 13 Harley Street, just one block away from Mansfield Street where the Persian ambassador was lodged. See Cloake 1988: 121.

Fig. 15. At least eight portraits of Mirza 'Abu'l Hasan Khan Shirazi were done during his two visits to Europe. Sir William Beechey's first portrait of the Persian envoy shows the painter's consummate skill in depicting the richly patterned silk brocade worn by his subject. Like 'Askar Khan, Mirza 'Abu'l Hasan Khan Shirazi wears a fur-trimmed cloak. In addition to a beautiful kamarband, he sports a black leather belt studded with gold and silver (?) plaques.

good enough to come to his studio for two hours each day, in the early morning.'[64] The resultant full-length portrait of the Persian ambassador (Fig. 15), shown wearing a sumptuous garment with a patterned, fur-trimmed cloak and elaborate Cashmere shawl for a turban, was exhibited at the Royal Academy, beginning on 27 April, 1810,[65] and was later hung in East India House. It was subsequently transferred to the Foreign and Commonwealth Office, Whitehall,[66] and currently hangs in the India Office Library.[67] Mirza 'Abu'l Hasan Khan Shirazi's right hand rests on a folded document, perhaps a copy of the Anglo-Persian treaty he had come to London to see ratified.

At about the same time as Beechey was probably finishing the Persian ambassador's portrait, Mirza 'Abu'l Hasan Khan Shirazi's diary records a visit to the studio of John Bacon, Jr.[68] on 27 March, 1810. After arriving and marveling at 'an image of the Minister for Foreign Affairs which was so good it seemed that the stone was alive and the Minister himself was with us....Sir Gore Ouseley then explained that the reason for taking me to visit the sculptor was that he wanted a bust of me to take with him to Iran. I am to return in a week's time so that the master can begin the work.'[69] In fact, Bacon is known to have completed two busts of Mirza 'Abu'l Hasan Khan Shirazi, neither of which appears to have survived, although one was exhibited at the Royal Academy in 1811.[70]

---

64. Cloake 1988: 121. The East India Company purchased the portrait in August, 1810.

65. Graves 1905: 162, s.v. 1810. 42 The Persian Ambassador.

66. Cloake 1988: 121.

67. Levey 2005: 152.

68. Millard 1967: 119. Bacon and his father are best known for creating numerous Anglo-Indian monuments in 'the decorative allegorical style characterizing much of mid- to late-eighteenth century British sculpture.' According to Groseclose 1995: 11, 'The younger Bacon probably created more works for the Presidency cities than anyone else, and many of them provided startling glimpses of his own exuberant talent.' These included the 1805 monument to James Achilles Kirkpatrick in St. John's Church, Calcutta; an 1807 monument to the German Lutheran missionary Christian Friedrich Schwartz in Madras (Chennai); and the 1815 monument to Lieut. Peter Lawrie in St. John's Church, Calcutta; see Groseclose 1995: 68, 91, 101. Because of his strong Christian beliefs and adherence to the missionizing function of the East India Company Bacon is considered an 'Evangelical sculptor.' See Atkins 2019: 208. In 1799 Bacon and his father together sculpted the monument to the renowned Orientalist, Persian and Sanskrit scholar, Sir William Jones in St. Paul's Cathedral, London, which appears on the cover of Edwards and Burnage 2017.

69. Cloake 1988: 183.

70. See Graves 1905: 88, s.v. 1811. 909 Bust of Persian Ambassador.

Beechey's second portrait (Fig. 16) of the Persian ambassador was very
different from the first, and it is unclear exactly when he did it. In this work,
Mirza 'Abu'l Hasan Khan Shirazi is kneeling, resting on his haunches, and
wears a much less elaborate dress consisting of a pale grey-blue under garment,
with a simple red cloak over his shoulders. His Cashmere shawl turban is much
the same as he always wore. The sitter's head is shown in profile, although his
torso faces the viewer. The portrait was sold to Compton Verney House at the
Christie's sale of 7 June, 2006 (lot 50).[71]

That this work was painted shortly before the ambassador's departure from
England in July, 1810, is strongly suggested by its close resemblance to a
miniature portrait by Beechey's wife, the accomplished miniaturist Lady Anne
Beechey.[72] Mirza Abu'l Hasan Khan is dressed in the exact same garment in
the two portraits, but the angle of his head and the exposure of his undershirt,
the placement of the decoration on the turban, and the line of the cloak falling
off of his shoulders are just slightly different in each case. It seems reasonable
to assume that both portraits were done during the same sitting(s). The back of
the miniature has two handwritten notes. The upper one reads, 'Presented by
Adml Ld Radstock[73] to Elizabeth Laura Countess of Waldegrave Augt 15th 1811,'
while the lower reads, 'The Portrait of Mirza Abul Hassan Envoy Extraordinary
from the King of Persia to the Court of Great Britain. The resemblance is most
striking, and was painted by Lady Beechey just previous to the Mirza's departure.
July 1810. Radstock.' Elizabeth Laura was one of the four children of Horace
Walpole's (1717-1797) brother Edward by Dorothy Clement, his mistress. She
and her siblings spent a great deal of time at Walpole's residence, Strawberry
Hill. Following Walpole's death, when the contents of his house were sold at

---

71. https://www.christies.com/en/lot/lot-4718893.

72. A portrait painter in her own right who had exhibited at the Royal Academy as early as
    1787 under the name Miss A.P. Jessop. See Millard 1967: Fig. 5.

73. Admiral Lord Radstock (William Waldegrave [1763–1825]) was a distant cousin of
    Countess Elizabeth Waldegrave (1760–1816). See Longmate 1810: 335.

Fig. 16. Beechey's second portrait of Mirza 'Abu'l Hasan Khan Shirazi captures a much more intimate moment, as if the ambassador were in the privacy of his own apartments. A simple grey tunic, with a red robe, lined with green velvet, contrast markedly with the rich dress seen in Fig. 15. The ambassador clutches a small book in his right hand, his forefinger holding his place in the text. With his head in profile, Mirza 'Abu'l Hasan's expression is relaxed, almost as if he were pictured in the act of listening to an unseen friend telling him a story.

auction in the Great Sale of 1842,[74] the miniature was 'bought in,' i.e. left unsold, and it remains to this day in the Waldegrave collection.[75]

Yet another portrait of Mirza 'Abu'l Hasan Khan Shirazi (Fig. 17) was painted in June/July, 1810, as well. The Persian ambassador's diary entry for 3 June, 1810, records that he and Sir Gore Ouseley went to the home of Sir Thomas Lawrence.

> Sir Gore Ouseley told me that he is the best portrait painter in London and that he wants him to paint my portrait to take with him to Iran. When we saw some 500 unfinished portraits of distinguished ladies and gentlemen, I exclaimed that mine would never be finished if we were to leave in ten days' time! Sir Gore Ouseley made it clear to the artist that if the portrait was not finished by the time we left, he would not be paid! It was finally agreed that he would paint a small portrait — from head to waist — and that I should return in three days' time to sit for him.[76]

The diary records a sitting on 6 June, noting also that 'Sir Gore Ouseley had given him [Lawrence] seventy *tomans*[77] to paint a half-length portrait of me — a good painter charges between 150 and 500 *tomans* for a full-length portrait.'[78] Mirza 'Abu'l Hasan Khan Shirazi sat again for Lawrence on 13 and 26 June[79] and the painting was certainly finished by 14 July 14, 1810, when Sir Gore Ouseley and Mirza 'Abu'l Hasan Khan Shirazi left London for Portsmouth, prior to boarding the *Lion* on 18 July for their return journey, via Brazil, to Tehran where Ouseley was being sent as Ambassador Extraordinary and Plenipotentiary.[80] The

---

74. See the sale catalogue Anonymous 1842: 148, s.v. lot 102, A miniature Portrait of Mirza Abal Hassan, Envoy Extraordinary from the King of Persia, painted by Lady Beechey, presented by Admiral Lord Radstock to Elizabeth Laura, Countess of Waldegrave, August 15, 1811. The miniatures went up for sale on the fourteenth day of the auction, Tuesday, 10 May, 1842.

75. Millard 1967: 121, n. 38.

76. Cloake 1967: 254.

77. For the value, c. £70, see Anonymous 1896: 369. Converting this price into today's dollars is potentially very misleading as it depends entirely on the price of gold and silver, as well as the quantity of each in the British pound and the United States dollar of the time. See e.g. Seaman 1852: 242.

78. Cloake 1967: 257.

79. Cloake 1967: 264, 275.

80. For the dates see Reynolds 1846: xlviii. Cf. Vahdat 2017: Appendix A; Ekbal 1987: 23.

Fig. 17. Sir Thomas Lawrence painted Mirza 'Abu'l Hasan Khan Shirazi's portrait shortly before the ambassador returned to Iran in company with Sir Gore Ouseley. While the envoy is dressed formally his expression, and arched eyebrows, give his face both an air of realism and intimacy, suggesting a thoughtful mind beneath the elaborate turban. The dark palette of this work adds an element of gravity and dignity, notwithstanding the ambassador's relaxed attitude. Both Lawrence and his admirers considered this one of the best portraits he ever did.

length of time it took Lawrence to complete the portrait is, however, complicated by a letter of 26 January, 1830, sent by Ouseley to D.E. Williams, who edited Lawrence's correspondence after his death. In it Ouseley noted that, 'I am proud to think, from a kindly feeling to myself, Sir Thomas Lawrence contrived, in the short space of seventy-four days, to finish a beautiful portrait of his Excellency, that is generally considered, not only an excellent likeness, but one of the best pictures he ever painted. Indeed, he was himself so proud of it, that, on my return from Persia in 1815, he made me promise never to let anyone but himself clean or varnish it.'[81] If, as implied by the entries in Mirza 'Abu'l Hasan Khan Shirazi's diary, the portrait was begun on 6 June and completed before 14 July, then it only took a maximum of 38, not 74 days.

The same letter provides fascinating insight into the Persian Prime Minister's reaction to Lawrence's portrait when he first encountered it in Ouseley's residence in Tehran, as well as giving some idea of what a viewer, not used to the genre of Western portraiture, made of such an image. Ouseley wrote:

> His Excellency Mirza Shefi, prime minister of the king of Persia, called upon me one morning at Tehran, so unexpectedly, that I had not time to remove the Persian ambassador's portrait from the sofa, on which I had placed it the moment before, from out of its packing case. I hastened to the door of the drawing-room to receive the minister, and taking him by the hand, was leading him to the sofa, when he unaccountably drew back. It is necessary to premise, that in Persian houses, (and I was then living in a palace lent me by the king, whilst my own was building,) the apartments have frequently open windows as well as doors of communication to other rooms on the same floor, and that Mirza Shefi may have possibly mistaken the frame of the picture, erect against the wall, for that of a window. At all events it did not injure the illusion. On looking back to learn the cause of his hesitation, I perceived the old minister's countenance inflamed with anger, which, before I could inquire the cause of it, burst forth in an apostrophe to the portrait. 'I think,' said he; 'that when the representative of the King of England does me the honour of standing up to receive me, in due respect to him, you should not be seated.' I could not resist laughing at this delightful mistake, and before I could explain, he said to me, 'Yes, it is your Excellency's kindness to that impertinent fellow that encourages such disrespect, but with your permission I'll soon teach him to know his distance.' Shaking his cane at the picture, he

---

81. Williams 1831: 55.

uttered a volley of abuse at poor Mirza Abul Hassan, and said, that if he
had forgotten all proper respect to Sir Gore Ouseley, he must at least show
it to the representative of his own sovereign. His rage was most violent, and
I was obliged to bring him close to the picture before he was undeceived.…
On approaching the picture, he passed his hand over the canvas, and, with
a look of unaffected surprise, exclaimed, 'Why! it has a flat surface!!
Yet at a little distance, I could have sworn by the Koran, that it was a
projecting substance — in truth, that it was Abul Hassan Khan himself.'[82]

Lawrence's portrait was later rendered as an engraving by John Lucas, who
produced a mezzotint with etching in 1835.[83] This was one of fifty-one mezzo-
tints included in a folio of Lawrence's works published after his death.[84] Since
1964 it has been in the collection of the Harvard Art Museum/Fogg Museum.[85]

In 1815 Mirza 'Abu'l Hasan Khan Shirazi was sent to St. Petersburg. Although
this proved to be a futile attempt to reverse some of the territorial losses suffered
by Persia in the First Russo-Persian War and to amend the boundaries that had
been fixed according to the 1813 Treaty of Golestan, the trip did offer yet another
opportunity for a portrait. In 1825, at its annual exhibition, the Pennsylvania
Academy of the Fine Arts displayed renowned Polish lithographer Alexander
Osipovich Orlowski's[86] (1777–1832) portrait done when the Persian ambassador's was in St. Petersburg.[87] This print, however, must have been loaned for
the exhibition by a private collector in Philadelphia for it never entered the
Academy's own collection.[88] The arrival of the Persian ambassador was also

---

82. Williams 1831: 55–58.

83. One of these is held by the National Galleries Scotland (P 8974; H: 11", W: 8 1/2"). See
    https://www.nationalgalleries.org/art-and-artists/24720/mirza-abul-hassan-khan.

84. Engravings from Anonymous 1835. Ffteen other artists besides Lucas were responsible
    for the engravings. See Anonymous 1899: 415.

85. For the portrait see e.g. Millard 1967: Pl. III; Levey 2005: 152.

86. Also Orlovsky, Orlovskii.

87. Falk 1988: 418, 'Mirza Abdoul Hassan Kahn, Persian ambassador, A. O. Orlowski, 1825.'

88. My thanks to Hoang Tran, Director of Archives, Pennsylvania Academy of the Fine
    Arts, for this information.

Fig. 18. The portrait of Mirza 'Abdul Hoseyn Khan Shirazi, done in Vienna by the Austrian miniaturist Moritz Michael Daffinger, has an almost photographic quality about it. In part this is due to the stillness of the pose, reminiscent of early daguerreotype portraiture. Moreover, although the fur-trimmed cloak is only lightly sketched in, the stunning depiction of the texture of the envoy's black lambskin cap, and the visible elements of the decorations worn, add a degree of realism that is striking. The treatment of the hair, protruding from beneath the cap, the beard and moustache, all add to the lifelike character of this portrait.

recorded in a mezzotint by Alexey Saltykov.[89] It has not been possible to trace an image of this portrait.

Three years later Mirza Abu'l Hasan Khan Shirazi was sent on another foreign mission. He and his nephew Mirza 'Abdul Hoseyn Khan Shirazi, whom Fath 'Ali Shah had appointed as his first ambassador to Vienna, departed on 21 May, 1818.[90] They travelled overland, via Constantinople, to Vienna, where Mirza 'Abu'l Hasan Khan Shirazi left his nephew before continuing on to Paris and eventually London. In Vienna the prominent Austrian miniaturist Moritz Michael Daffinger (1790–1849) painted a miniature portrait of Mirza 'Abdul Hoseyn Khan Shirazi[91] (Fig. 18) which belonged to Princess Melanie, *née* Zichy-Ferraris (1805–1854), the wife of the long-serving Austrian Foreign Minister, Prince Klemens Wenzel Lothar von Metternich (1773–1859), who amassed a collection of over 150 of Daffinger's watercolor and miniature portraits and was, together with her husband, one of the artist's greatest patrons.[92] The collection was exhibited at the Art History Museum (Metternichschen Sammlung, Kunsthistorisches Hofmuseum) and in 2012 was sold at auction.[93] The portrait of Mirza 'Abdul

---

89. Alexey Saltykov, *Entry into St. Petersburg of the Persian Ambassador*, done prior to December 23, 1815. Watercolor on paper (H: 7", W: 8 2/10"). See Petrova 2004: 20. Saltykov belonged to an extended family that 'occupied a dominant position in military administration, the police, and financial administration.' See Le Donne 1987: 237.

90. According to Hasan-e Fasa'i, Mirza Abu'l Hasan Khan Shirazi brought with him 'presents befitting kings.' See Busse 1972: 155. These included a portrait of Fath 'Ali Shah set in a frame of Chinese jade. See Montbel 1832: 80, 'Parmi ces objets précieux…on remarquait le portrait du monarque persan, encadré d'une riche bordure, en pierre de jade de la Chine.' Describing the miniature, which was presented to the Emperor on a cushion, Payer von Thurn 1907: 18, wrote, 'Auf der ersten Sänfte lag das Porträt des Schahs, auf einer Platte aus Milch-Chalcedon emailliert, mit Spinellen rund herum besetzt, und ein Kranz großer Perlen, dem Medaillon zur Einfassung dienend' ('On the first cushion lay the portrait of the Shah, enamelled on a flat piece of milk chalcedony, set all around with spinels, and a crown of pearls serving to secure the medallion'). The two ambassadors had their audience on 8 February, 1819.

91. Payer von Thurn 1907: 18, n. 1. See Weckbecker 1902: 285. For his life and work in general see Leo Grünstein 1923.

92. In her diary, under September, 1849, Princess Melanie noted, 'Le peintre Daffinger est mort. C'était un brave homme plein de talent, auquel je dois ma collection de portraits.' See Metternich 1884: 66.

93. See Anonymous 2012: 95, no. 147. The description given there is incorrect as it dated the ambassador's stay to February-March, 1839, rather than 1819. In fact, he was in Vienna from 1-21 February, 1819, according to Payer von Thurn 1907: 18. Cf. Höflechner and Wagner 2011: 1446, n. 1431.

Hoseyn Khan Shirazi was acquired by the Metropolitan Museum of Art.[94] The Qajar court historian Hasan-e Fasa'i noted the return of Mirza 'Abdul Hoseyn Khan Shiraz, at an unspecified date in 1819, 'who had been sent on a mission to Austria, carrying a letter of friendship and presents from the Austrian emperor.'[95]

While in Vienna Mirza 'Abu'l Hasan Khan Shirazi also had his portrait drawn by Peter Fendi (1796–1842),[96] one of the most important Austrian artists of the early 19th century. Like Toulouse-Lautrec, he was small in stature and disabled, although the exact nature of his condition is unclear. His intimate depictions of group scenes of the Austrian royal family were unprecedented. In his 1832 portrait of Emperor Franz I he drew on a Baroque tradition of rulers' portraits, with the addition of 19th century realism.[97] In addition to 'Fendi del.,' i.e. 'Fendi delineavit' or 'Fendi drew it,' which appears beneath Mirza 'Abu'l Hasan Khan Shirazi's torso, on the left, the words 'Versuch eines Stein Farben Druckes' appears on the right. Thus, this was an 'attempt at a color lithograph,'[98] and although the reproduction of Fendi's portrait in Payer von Thurn's article was not in color, it is not surprising that Fendi was experimenting at this time with

---

94. The date given for the portrait on the museum website, 1839, is incorrect. This may have been the date at which the portrait entered Princess Melanie's collection. A journal entry of hers from 28 November, 1836, appears to note the first portrait of Daffinger's acquired by her. See Anonymous 2012: 3. This being the case, it is conceivable that the portrait of the Persian ambassador was acquired in 1839, even though it had been painted two decades earlier. Alternatively, the portrait may have been a copy made by Daffinger for Princess Melanie of an original done in 1819.

95. Busse 1972: 159.

96. The portrait is unpaginated and appears between pages 20 and 21 in Payer von Thurn 1907. Unfortunately the quality of the scanned journal is too poor to permit inclusion here. It is entitled 'S[eine]. E[xzellenz]. Mirsa Abul Hassan Chan' and was described as a collotype from the Königlich und Kaiserlich Graphische Lehr- und Versuchsanstalt by Payer von Thurn 1907: 24. For the history of this institution, founded in 1888, see Matzer 2015: 28–56. For Fendi's life and career see Bergmann 1844; Wurzbach 1858: 173–175; Koschatzky 1995.

97. Schultes 2002: 65-66.

98. Groschwitz 1954: 243 distinguished between color lithography and chromolithography as follows: 'Etymologically and technically they are identical, but usage has assigned to chromolithography those unfortunately bad copies of paintings made by this process, which are popularly referred to as chromos....To make the distinction, then, a color lithograph is an original, independent work of art that does not seek to imitate a watercolor or painting, but, rather, competes with them as a picture in printed form. It is conceived primarily in terms of color, of which black may be one, and is drawn on stone.'

color lithography. As Krause noted, the development of color lithography was, at least in part, stimulated by Immanuel Kant's (1724–1804) 1790 treatise *Critique of Aesthetic Judgement* which emphasized the fact that, while drawing was of fundamental importance in all of the arts — painting, sculpture, architecture, landscape architecture — 'colors, that illuminate an outline, confer charm.'[99] Yet as Krause has detailed, the technical difficulties of color lithography took years to overcome. Innovations and small improvements were made in France in 1816–1818 and Fendi was experimenting in this field, together with the Viennese lithographer Josef Lanzedelly the Elder (1774-1832), in 1819.[100] Hence, Fendi's description of his color lithograph of Mirza 'Abu'l Hasan Khan Shirazi as an 'attempt' (Versuch) places the work squarely within this experimental effort. Truly successful color lithography was only achieved much later. While some scholars considered Manet's *Polichinelle* (1876) 'the first true color lithograph,' others conferred this title on a much earlier landscape by Auguste Bouquet (1810-1846) and Émile Lessore (1805-1876) in the Metropolitan Museum of Art, dated to 1837.[101] That Fendi was technically very advanced, or at least adventurous, is shown by the fact that his color lithograph was made using eight stones. For comparison, the Bouquet and Lessore color lithograph of 1837 only used four stones while Manet's *Polichinelle* of 1876 employed seven.[102]

Fendi's portrait shows Mirza 'Abu'l Hasan Khan Shirazi in a typical tall, black sheepskin hat, appropriate for the time of year (February), from the front of which a pendant of sorts is suspended. The small size of the central plaque, mounted in a large disc with what appear to be eight round elements around the edge, suggests that this could be a decoration. On the other hand, the shape does not correspond to early Qajar decorations, and it may have been an Austrian order given to him during his visit to Vienna, in the shape of the sun, with the portrait of the Austrian Emperor, Franz I (r. 1804–1835), in the center, as described by

---

99. 'In der Malerei, Bildhauerkunst, ja allen bildenden Künsten, in der Baukunst, Gartenkunst, ist die Zeichnung das Wesentliche, in welcher nicht, was in der Empfindung vergnügt, sondern bloß was durch seine Form gefällt, den Grund aller Anlage für den Geschmack ausmacht. Die Farben, welche den Abriß illuminieren, gehören zum Reiz....Der Reiz der Farben, aber die Zeichnung in der ersten und die Komposition in dem letzten machen den eigentlichen Gegenstand des reinen Geschmackurteils aus.' See Helmut H. Krause 2007: 76.

100. Krause 2007: 78.

101. Groschwitz 1954: 246–247.

102. Groschwitz 1954: 246–248.

Goethe.[103] Mirza 'Abu'l Hasan Khan Shirazi wears a cloak decorated all over in a paisley pattern; a patterned garment beneath; a sash across his chest; and a Cashmere shawl *kamarband* from which the hilt of a dagger protrudes.

When Mirza 'Abu'l Hasan Khan Shirazi reached Paris he was sketched by an even more illustrious artist, Eugène Delacroix (1798–1863), who made a full-length drawing of him[104] which was turned into a lithograph (Fig. 19) by Charles-Philibert Comte de Lasteyrie (1759–1849), the real founder of lithography in France, after an unsuccessful introduction of the technology by Johann Anton André (1741–1799),[105] who had himself gone to Munich in 1812 to learn the technique, only to have his plans interrupted by Napoleon's Russian campaign. Lasteyrie returned to Munich again in 1814 and 'mastered every stage of the art from the polishing of stones to the pulling of proofs.' It was at this time, moreover, that he hired craftsmen and purchased equipment with which to establish his own lithographic establishment in Paris.[106] Delacroix's portrait is far less detailed, both in the depiction of the dress as well as the facial features (and the beard is minimal), than most of the other portraits considered here. Nor is the dress comparable. Apart from the fact that he clutches his sword, it is almost as if Mirza 'Abu'l Hasan Khan Shirazi had been caught in a private moment, *en déshabillé*, before completing his dressing. It is interesting to note that, two years earlier, in 1817, Delacroix, who had a well-known fascination with the East, had devoted some of his time to copying Persian miniatures.[107]

The lithograph of a second portrait (Fig. 20) done in Paris is held by the Bibliothèque National in Paris. It is inscribed with the legend 'S[on]. E[xcellence]. Mirza Aboul Hassan-Khan, Présenté à S[a]. M[ajesté]. Louis XVIII. Le 30 Mars 1819.' In addition, beneath the portrait, which ends just above the

---

103. Goethe wrote, 'kaum ist er in Wien angelangt, so ereilen ihn glänzende Bestätigungen seiner Würde, affallende Zeugnisse seiner Bedeutung. Eine Fahne mit Insignien des Reichs wird ihm gesendet, ein Ordensband mit dem Gleichniß der Sonne, ja mit dem Ebenbild des Kaisers selbst verziert: das alles erhebt ihn zum Stellvertreter der höchsten Macht, in und mit ihm ist die Majestät gegenwärtig.' See Goethe 1867: 267. Goethe also wrote a poem about Mirza 'Abu'l Hasan Khan Shirazi's wearing of the Order of the Lion and Sun entitled 'Auf das Ordensband mit dem Bilde der Sonne und des Königes.'

104. Moreau 1873: 27, H: 11", W. 7 ½", *L'Ambassadeur de Perse*; Robaut, Chesneau and Calmettes 1885: 6.

105. See Motte 1831: 238. Cf. Gauzente and Pascaud 2018. For Motte's lithographic portrait of Mirza 'Abu'l Hasan Khan Shirazi, see below.

106. See Pennell and Pennell 1898: 40.

107. Sjöberg 1963: 100.

S. Ex. Mirza Aboul hassan Khan
Ambassadeur de Perse

Fig. 19. Charles-Philibert Comte de Lasteyrie turned a drawing by Delacroix into this lithographic portrait of Mirza 'Abu'l Hasan Khan Shirazi during the Persian envoy's second visit to Europe. Most of the attention in this work seems to have gone into the rendering of the dress, which looks more Indian than Persian, whereas the ambassador's high forehead, raised eyebrows, and knotted turban, are almost caricature-like.

chez Martinet.   *Lithog.^{the} de C. Motte*

S. E. Mirza Aboul-Hassan-Khan,
Présenté à S. M. Louis XVIII. Le 30 mars 1819.

Fig. 20. The identity of the artist responsible for this portrait is unknown. The legend on the lithgraph identifies only the name of the lithographer, Charles Motte, and the publisher, Martinet. In contrast to the portraits executed during Mirza 'Abu'l Hasan Khan Shirazi's first visit to Europe, this one is highly stylized, particularly in the rendering of the beard. The presence of several decorations worn by the ambassador attests to the fact that he had risen in the world since his first embassy to England several years earlier.

waist, there appears, on the left, 'chez Martinet,' and, on the right, 'Lithog.[ie] de C. Motte.' The origins of the venerable publishing house of Martinet date to 1694. In 1798 Aaron Martinet (1762–1841) founded an enormously successful and popular shopfront in the rue du Coq (now rue Marengo), near the Louvre,[108] and by the late 19th century it employed over 400 people and was described as one of the oldest and most important of the great Parisian publishers.[109] Charles Motte (1785–1836) was a lithographer located in the rue des Marais, Fauxbourg St.-Germain. After Lasteyrie, Motte was one of the leading lithographers in Paris, winning silver medals at the expositions of French industry in 1823, 1827 and 1834.[110] His association with Delacroix[111] is interesting in light of the fact that both were responsible for lithographed portraits of Mirza 'Abu'l Hasan Khan Shirazi.

The Motte lithograph appears to have been drawn with a Conté crayon. It is unclear whether Motte himself drew the portrait which, apart from the face, is characterized by a loose, sketchy feel. Mirza 'Abu'l Hasan Khan Shirazi wears a patterned garment, with a sash across his right shoulder and chest. A dagger with a jewel-encrusted hilt sits in his *kamarband*. Two decorations and a jewelled brooch are shown. One, beribboned, facetted star-shaped decoration, worn on the chest, is unquestionably an Order of the Lion and the Sun, 1st Class (Grand Cordon), which had been instituted by Fath 'Ali Shah about a decade earlier. The enamelled plaque in the center would show 'the Sun rising upon the back of the Lion, or the Sun in Leo, i.e., the Sun in its fullest power in the zodiac,' which is more visible on a slightly later portrait by Massimo Gauci (see below). Another decoration is shown suspended from the ambassador's turban. The ribbon from which it hangs appears to be tucked into the folds of the turban. This order resembles the circular disc-shaped order identified above as one given to Mirza 'Abu'l Hasan Khan Shirazi in Vienna by the Emperor. To the left is what appears to be an ornate brooch, encrusted with pearls and semi-precious stones, topped by a floral, stem-like element.

The Persian ambassador reached London on 27 April, 1819, and took up residence in a house in Charles Street, Berkeley Square.[112] His visit yielded

---

108. McPhee and Orenstein 2011: 12–14.

109. Anonymous 1882.

110. Engelmann 1840: 447–448. He has been called one of the most important lithographers of the early 19th century. See Würtenberger 2017: 277.

111. See e.g. Anonymous 1974: 21; Néret 2000: 30.

112. Paton 1838: 304.

Drawn by the Hon.ᵇˡᵉ Miss E.   Engraved by G.Bartolozzi.

Fig. 21. The Honorable Miss E., most probably Emily Eden, drew Mirza 'Abu'l Hasan
Khan Shirazi seated on a sofa, his left foot resting on a low footstool. The proportions
of the figure in the drawing are incorrect, as can be seen by comparing the envoy's large
hands with his relatively small head. The Bartolozzis were well-known engravers in
London and had a close relationship with Paul Colnaghi, whose firm printed the portrait.

three more portraits, none of which was as exalted as those executed nine years earlier by Beechey and Lawrence. Shortly after his arrival, Mirza 'Abu'l Hasan Khan Shirazi's portrait (Fig. 21) was drawn by 'the Hon[bl] Miss E.,' an engraving of which, entitled 'Mirza Abul Hassan Envoy Extraordinary from the King of Persia,' was done by Gaetano Stefano Bartolozzi (1757–1821) and published in London on 1 May, 1819, by Messrs. Colnaghi & Co., 23 Cockspur Street. Given the style and the date it is extremely likely that 'Miss E.' was Emily Eden (1797-1869), sister of George Lord Auckland, later Governor-General of India, and a prolific artist who produced a striking series of portraits of Indian princes when she was in India as her brother's consort from 1836 to 1842.[113] Son of the famed Francesco Bartolozzi (1727–1815),[114] Gaetano Bartolozzi is much less well known. In fact, his father's biographer said that his works were 'few in number,' and could only name a handful of portraits engraved by him.[115] In the present instance, it would seem that the name must have been attached to the former Bartolozzi workshop for in 1797 Gaetano had sold his father's stock of copperplates and moved to Paris, where he opened a fencing and music academy and died in 1821.[116] Thus, it is unlikely that this was actually Bartolozzi's work, and more probable that it was a product of the workshop that continued to bear his name after his move to Paris.[117] Francesco Bartolozzi's relationship with the Milanese printer and art dealer Paul Colnaghi (1751-1833) dated to 1776, and it is therefore not surprising that an etching from the Bartolozzi workshop should have been printed by Colnaghi & Co.[118]

In contrast to most of the other portraits of Mirza 'Abu'l Hasan Khan Shirazi, the one by 'the Honorable Miss E.' shows him in a much more simplified dress, dominated by a long, fur-trimmed cloak. The ambassador is seated, his left foot resting on a stool. The stipple technique for which the Bartolozzi school was so famous is used to full effect, offering a subtle means of indicating patterning in

---

113. Eden 1844; Relia 2014: 66-73. For her life and work see Prior 2011; Ikeda 2019b: 2-3.

114. See e.g. Brinton 1906; Bally 1907.

115. Tuer 1885: 55–56.

116. Tuer 1885: 54.

117. As Bally 1907: xxviii wrote of Francsco, 'Bartolozzi was the head of a great school of stipple engraving, and it is almost certain that many of his prints to which he put his signature contained but little of the master's own engraving.' The signature of G. Bartolozzi on the etching of this portrait suggests that, even after Gaetano decamped to Paris, his name continued in use at his former workshop in London.

118. For the firm see e.g. Garstang 1984.

the turban, garment and cloak. Missing are any signs of elevated status — no decorations, jewelry or richly patterned textiles.

Although Mirza 'Abu'l Hasan Khan Shirazi arrived in London in late April, he was unable to have an audience with the Prince Regent until 20 May because the Prince was indisposed. A profile equestrian 'portrait' of Mirza Abu'l Hasan Khan Shirazi by the satirist Richard Dighton (1795–1880), dating to the same month, was presumably drawn from life while the ambassador was taking some exercise in London. It is scarcely a portrait, and more attention has been paid to the horse than its rider.[119]

A more formal, three-quarter length portrait, dated 12 July, 1819, was done by the Maltese-born lithographer Massimo (Maxim) Gauci (1774-1854).[120] In it (Fig. 22) Mirza 'Abu'l Hasan Khan Shirazi wears a decoration and a brooch. The decoration, in the form of an eight-pointed star with enameled image in the center, appears to be the Order of the Lion and Sun, discussed above. In addition, Mirza 'Abu'l Hasan Khan Shirazi wears a painted enamel or porcelain portrait of Fath 'Ali Shah, his sovereign, suspended from a velvet ribbon around his neck. The portrait is housed in an elaborate setting with ten strings of pendant diamonds.[121] This particular portrait of Fath 'Ali Shah was based on one done by Sir Robert Ker Porter (1777–1842) while visiting Tehran in May, 1818.[122] An

---

119. For a copy in the National Portrait Gallery (London), entitled 'His Excellency the Persian Ambassador,' hand-colored etching. H: 12 1/8", W: 10", see https://www.npg. org.uk/collections/search/portrait/mw64904/Mirza-Abdul-Hassan-Khan-Ilci-His-Excellency-the-Persian-Ambassador?

120. Millard 1967: Fig. 1. The lithographed portrait bears a label that reads 'Painted from Nature & Drawn on Stone by M. Gauci Esq.' See https://collections.vam.ac.uk/item/ O1107117/his-excellency-mirza-abul-hassan-lithograph-gauci/. Gauci is recognized as 'a pioneering botanical lithographer' who 'made almost three-hundred hand-colored lithograph plates after drawings by India[n] artists of the Calcutta Garden [Royal Botanic Garden, Calcutta]. See O'Malley 2014: 66. His work features heavily in the plates published in Royle 1839. Gauci was also known as the 'father of music hall artists' in view of his extensive body of engraved and hand-colored sheet music. See Hall 1981: 3. Describing Gauci's lithographs, Walker 1852: xii, called 'Mr. M. Gauci, the first of our lithographers, equally distinguished by correct anatomical knowledge, learning in ancient art, and exquisite taste.'

121. For another example which, however, lacks the pendant diamonds, see https://www. bonhams.com/auctions/21722/lot/156/. Cf. one in the Nasser D. Khalili Collection of Islamic Art. See https://www.tate.org.uk/whats-on/tate-britain/exhibition/east-west-objects-between-cultures/east-west-room-6.

122. For the date see Barnett 1972: 21. On Ker Porter's life and career see also Armstrong 1962.

Fig. 22. The long legend at the bottom of Gauci's portrait of 'His Excellency Mirza Abul Hassan Khan Ambassador Extraordinary from his Majesty the Shah of Persia to H.R.H. the Prince Regent of Great Britain,' carries the dedication, 'To His Excellency Sir Gore Ouseley Bart. KLS KAS late Ambassador Extraordinary to the Court of Persia, this Lithographic Plate is respectfully dedicated (with permission) by his most humble Servant M. Gauci,' and is dated July 12th, 1819. Gauci's work may not be the most compelling image of the ambassador, but it is replete with detail, from the decorations worn in the turban and those on the ambassador's chest, to the beautifully rendered ceremonial sword, jewel-encrusted dagger, and belt.

engraving of the portrait was published in 1822 as the frontispiece of the first volume of his account of his travels.[123] A second, ornately framed miniature, just below the left arm, appears to hang from the green velvet sash worn over Mirza 'Abu'l Hasan Khan Shirazi's right shoulder and across his chest.

The Gauci portrait differs from those of Beechey and Lawrence in several interesting respects. While Mirza 'Abu'l Hasan Khan Shirazi wore a sumptuous, golden garment and fur-trimmed cloak in the portraits of 1810, he was attired in a much less ornate, patterned garment in 1819. For Gauci, however, he wore his official regalia, not only his decoration and the portrait brooch, described above, but a much more colorful Cashmere shawl turban adorned with a diamond and pearl, feather-like pin, and a second gold pendant, hanging from a chain, with pendant tear-drop, semi-precious stones. The hilt of his dagger is encrusted with what appear to be rubies, and his belt, too, is studded with baguette-cut sapphires. When he returned to London in 1819, Mirza 'Abu'l Hasan Khan Shirazi was a far more experienced diplomat than he had been in 1810, and he seems clearly comfortable wearing the regalia that reflected his station.

In October, Mirza 'Abu'l Hasan Khan Shirazi left London with the intention of visiting Scotland and Ireland before returning home. He reached Dumbreck's Hotel in Edinburgh on 30 October, and moved soon afterwards to the Royal Hotel.[124] The prolific and much-loved Scottish miniaturist John Kay (1742-1828)[125] did a drawing of the ambassador that is more of a caricature than a portrait.[126] A former barber with a talent for drawing humorous and often satirical caricatures, Kay was an Edinburgh institution.[127] Hugh Paton (1806–1863), the compiler of Kay's works, is identified on the titlepage of the collected caricatures volume as 'Carver and Gilder to the Queen and Her R.H. the Duchess of Kent.'[128] Describing Mirza 'Abu'l Hasan Khan Shirazi's visit Paton observed, 'During his short stay in Edinburgh the attention he experienced from the public authorities, and others

---

123. Ker Porter 1821: unpaginated frontispiece.

124. Paton 1838: 307.

125. For his life and career, see Evans 1973.

126. Paton 1838: 300.

127. According to Thomson 1875: 415–416, 'He etched in all nearly nine hundred plates, forming a complete record of the public characters, of every grade and kind, including many distinguished strangers, who made a figure in Edinburgh for nearly half a century. It may be safely affirmed that no city in the empire can boast of so curious a chronicle.

128. 'Hugh Paton, *Mapping the Practice and Profession of Sculpture in Britain and Ireland 1851-1951*, University of Glasgow History of Art and HATII, online database 2011 [http://sculpture.gla.ac.uk/view/organization.php?id=msib6_1213615441, accessed 13 Jul 2021].

who attended him in his perambulations, called forth the most lively expressions of satisfaction. In the Print by Kay the Mirza is represented in his riding-dress.'[129]

MIRZA SALEH SHIRAZI

One of the very few, non-élite Persians whose portrait was done in London was Mirza Saleh Shirazi. He was among the five students sent in 1815 by the crown prince 'Abbas Mirza to learn useful trades in England. Mirza Saleh was meant to learn English and other languages, including French, in order to become a translator.[130] Previously he had been a secretary in the army of the crown prince. As Mirza Saleh's diary shows, however, he also became apprenticed to the printer and typefounder Richard Watts (d. 1844).[131] Mirza Saleh returned to Iran from England in July, 1823, but before leaving England a portrait bust of him was done by the sculptor and later inventor, Robert William Sievier (1794–1865). First displayed at the Royal Academy in 1823,[132] it is today in the Cultural Institute of Bonyad Museums, Tehran.[133] After his return to Iran Mirza Saleh accompanied Khosrow Mirza to St. Petersburg (see below) and was responsible for printing the first Iranian newspaper.[134]

KHOSROW MIRZA AND HIS COMPANIONS

We come next to the portraits of the sixteen year-old prince Khosrow Mirza who, in 1829, was sent to St. Petersburg with a large entourage to formally apologize for the brutal murder of the Russian ambassador, Alexander Sergeyevich Griboyedov (1795–1829), and nearly the entire Russian legation in Tehran by a violent mob.[135] Khosrow Mirza was a son of the crown prince 'Abbas Mirza, and grandson of Fath 'Ali Shah. Sending the young prince to tender the apology

---

129. Paton 1838: 308.

130. Atai 1992: 22.

131. Green 2014: 78, 80, 83, 87.

132. The catalogue entry reads, 'Bust, in Marble, of Mirza Sauleh.— R.W. Siever. This is a most singular and beautiful bust, exhibiting, particularly in the beard and cap, very fine tooling.' See Westmacott 1823: 23.

133. Vahdat 2017: Fig. 2.1.

134. See e.g. Vosoughi 2016: 1263-1271; Borna Izadpanah, 'The first Iranian Newspaper' (British Library Asian and African Studies Blog, July 18, 2019. https://blogs.bl.uk/asian-and-african/2019/07/the-first-iraniannewspaper-mirza-salih-shirazis-kaghaz-i-akhbar.html).

135. For the incident see e.g. Lang 1948: 317-339; Costello 1967: 52-73; Harden 1979; and Kelly 2006.

Fig. 23. The watercolor of Khosrow Mirza by Filipp Osipovich Berger is an unpretentious portrait of an inexperienced young man whose grandfather, Fath 'Ali Shah, and father, 'Abbas Mirza, had sent him to tender an apology for the massacre of the Russian ambassador and his suite in Tehran. The brushstrokes suggest that the work was done relatively quickly, and nothing formal or stylized was added to mark either the dignity of the teenage ambassador's office or the gravity of his mission. The youth sports a moustache, but is beardless. Curls of long hair protrude from under his black sheepskin cap, framing his face. Khosrow Mirza's dagger is as simple as his dress.

before the Russian emperor rather than a senior minister or the crown prince himself proved a stroke of genius for the teenager charmed St. Petersburg society, most particularly Nicholas I, and his mission was a resounding success.[136] While he was in St. Petersburg Khosrow Mirza's portrait was done at least three times.

The first portrait, a watercolor sketch (Fig. 23), is signed 'P. Berger' in a flamboyant, cursive hand. This is probably Filipp Osipovich Berger (Berzhe) (1783–1867),[137] about whom little is known. The portrait is unique, however, in that it is much more immediate and less formal than most of the other portraits considered here. It shows the young ambassador wearing the typical, tall, black sheepskin cap;[138] a simple, mauve garment;[139] and a *kamarband* with touches of blue, in which a dagger has been thrust. Khosrow Mirza's youth is typified by the absence of a beard, a feature found in all of the other portraits of Iranians painted abroad discussed here.

A second portrait (Fig. 24) was done by Karl von Hampeln [Karl Karlovich Gampeln, Charles de Hampeln] (1794–1880). Hampeln was both deaf and speech-impaired. Although born in Moscow, he was educated at the Kaiserlich Königliche Taubstummen-Institut (Imperial Royal Institute for the Deaf and Speech-Impaired). In 1815 Hampeln was introduced to Alexander I, while the Russian emperor attended the Congress of Vienna. The emperor subsidized Hampeln's further education and Hampeln moved to Moscow, and later St. Petersburg, where he had a successful career as a painter, engraver and teacher at the institute for the deaf and speech-impaired.[140] Hampeln signed his work, e.g. 'Gravé par Charles de Hampeln Sourd-muet;' 'Dessiné d'après Nature et Gravé à St.-Petersbourg par Charles de Hampeln Sourd-muet de l'Académie des beaux Arts et de l'Institut des Sourds-muets à Vienne;' or simply 'Hampeln Sourd-muet.'[141]

Hampeln's portrait shows Khosrow Mirza attired in nearly the identical manner to that shown in Berger's sketch. The principal embellishment here, however, is

---

136. For the mission see Bournoutian 2014.

137. See http://painters.artunion.ru/english.htm.

138. According to Idesbald 1833: 78, when Khosrow Mirza had his first audience with Nicholas I, 'Ce prince avait sur la tête ce vilain bonnet pointu en astrakan, que est pour les sectateurs d'Ali ce que le kahouk est pour ceux de Mahomet.'

139. As Idesbald 1833: 78, observed, 'Ce costume de Khosrev n'était riche que par la beauté des tissus, qui paraissaient fort ouvragés.'

140. See Busch 1902: 121, n. 3.

141. Rovinsky 1895: 150–151.

نواشاهزاده والاتبار کامکار خسرو میرزا سنه ۱۲۴۰ مطابق هجری

Fig. 24. Karl von Hampeln's portrait of Khosrow Mirza resembles that of Berger, with the exception of a more elaborate kamarband. This is not the imposing figure of a man like 'Askar Khan Afshar Urumi or Mirza Abu'l Hasan Khan Shirazi, both many years his senior when their portraits were painted. The expression on Khosrow Khan's clean-shaven face is thoughtful, the stare intent. The young prince is shown with a modest, somewhat wary, countenance.

the clearly patterned, Cashmere shawl *kamarband*, from which his dagger's hilt protrudes. Both this and the Berger portrait accentuate the young prince's dark curls which frame his youthful, albeit mustachioed face. Otherwise, Khosrow Mirza is dressed modestly, with little sign of royal pomp. In his short story 'The Portrait,' first published in 1835, Nikolai Gogol mentioned, amongst a group of engravings at a picture stall in the open-air market of Shchukin Dvor in St. Petersburg, 'a portrait of Khozrev-Mirza in a sheepskin hat.'[142] This certainly evokes the image of Hampeln's portrait.

A third portrait of Khosrow Mirza, currently untraceable, is said to have been painted by the Estonian painter and lithographer Gustav Adolph Hippius (1792–1856), from Reval (mod. Tallinn).[143] Like other Estonian artists, Hippius left his homeland at a relatively young age. Between 1812 and 1818 he spent time in Prague, Vienna, Munich, Augsburg, Venice, Mantua, Florence, Rome and Naples.[144] Before returning home he visited Switzerland where he drew what became the most famous portrait of the then 72 year old educational reformer, Johann Heinrich Pestalozzi (1746-1827), which was published as a lithograph in 1846 in celebration of his 100th birthday.[145] After remaining six months in Estonia, Hippius left again, in 1819, for St. Petersburg where he remained for over thirty years. He made a name for himself in 1822 with a series of lithographed portraits of leading statesmen, artists and intellectuals, but when he found himself unable to support himself through his artistic work alone, he turned to art education, particularly after the cholera epidemic of 1831 depressed the market for original works of art. After publishing his first collection of instructional material, accompanied by drawings made during his Italian sojourn, as *Le jeune dessinateur, cours d'études progressives à l'usage des écoles*, he brought out his *magnum opus* on the theory of drawing[146] which remained a standard text

---

142. English 1995: 62. Cf. the discussion in Maguire 1995: 143.

143. According to Melville 2013: 78, 'The prince commissioned several of his portraits from G.F. [sic] Gippius.'

144. Anonymous 1889: 713, 717; Anonymous 1890): 33; Anonymous 1890b: 116.

145. Anonymous 1890b: 121–122.

146. Hippius 1842. Cf. Kerbs, Lebede and Severin 1976: 53.

well into the late 19th century.[147] In 1848 Hippius was described as a 'portrait and history painter, currently drawing teacher' at various imperial educational institutions in St. Petersburg.'[148]

Finally, a fourth, lithographic portrait of Khosrow Mirza, by Adolph Friedrich Erdmann von Menzel, probably done in 1830 or 1831 and published in Berlin, was apparently not drawn from life.[149] It was probably based on Hampeln's, with some artistic license on Menzel's part.

While the Iranian mission was in St. Petersburg Hampeln did portraits of at least four other members of Khosrow Mirza's entourage, only two of which are illustrated here. These included Mirza Saleh (Fig. 25), whose earlier journey to England was discussed above. In 1829 Mirza Saleh was attached to Khosrow Mirza's mission in order to acquire a lithographic press in Russia. In fact, this turned out to be the first lithographic press imported into Iran. With it, the first Quran was printed in the country in 1832. The Persian legend beneath Hampeln's portrait, '*munshi-yi khas*,' identifies him as the chief secretary of Khosrow Mirza's father, crown prince 'Abbas Mirza.[150] Mirza Saleh's dress closely resembles that of Khosrow Mirza in Hampeln's portrait but, unusually, the aspiring printer is shown in profile. He too wears a black, sheepskin hat, from which locks of hair protrude, as well as a colorful *kamarband* with paisley figures clearly visible.

Mirza Baba, too, had his portrait done (Fig. 26). This was not Fath 'Ali Shah's court painter[151] but rather a namesake who, according to one source,[152] participated in Khosrow Mirza's embassy as the young prince's personal physician. Mirza Baba wears the obligatory black sheepskin cap and a coat with an embroidered or highly worked shawl colloar. His full but not overly dense beard, which descends nearly to his patterned *kamarband*, partially obscures a star-shaped decoration which adorns his chest. Finally, a third portrait of the eldest member of Khosrow

---

147. Anonymous 1890b: 127. Soon after its publication Hippius' *Grundlinien* was translated into Russian and was recommended to all art teachers in Russia by the Ministry of Education. It was also very popular in Germany.

148. Paucker 1848: 221.

149. *S[eine]r. Königl[icher]. Hoheit der Prinz Khosrow Mirza.* Described as a chalk lithograph on China paper (Kreidelithographie auf Chinapapier), H: 12 8/10", W: 9 6/10".

150. Green 2016: 310.

151. For whom see Floor 1999a: 140. He was active from c. 1785 to 1810.

152. 'Rußland,' *Der Oesterreichischer Beobachter* (Vienna, Austria), September 16, 1829. According to Idesbald 1833: 10, however, 'Un autre conseiller, Mirza Babba, d'une figure assez insignifiante, et ne sachant que quelques mots d'anglais, ne jouait dans le monde qu'un rôle fort secondaire.'

Fig. 25. Mirza Saleh's portrait by Karl von Hampeln shows him in profile, his posture erect and torso almost rigidly upright. The facial features, beard, mouth and hair protruding from beneath the black sheepskin cap have an air of almost photograph realism. The sitter, whose career is relatively well-documented, is most associated with the introduction of printing and lithography in Iran. Although he accompanied a royal Qajar prince on this journey, he is shown with no airs or accoutrements indicative of his participation in an important diplomatic undertaking.

Fig. 26. Khosrow Mirza's personal physician, Mirza Baba, is shown dressed modestly and in most respects resembles his comrades. Yet through the hair of his long beard we can clearly see a decoration worn on his chest, almost certainly conferred upon him by Fath 'Ali Shah. The patterned kamarband and decorated lapels of his coat are the only indications of status displayed by Mirza Baba's clothing. Hampeln's realistic portraits of Khosrow Mirza, Mirza Saleh and Mirza Baba are simple statements, divorced from the larger political concerns of the mission.

Mirza's entourage, not shown here, is that of Mirza Mas'ud, in three-quarter profile. This shows the subject dressed almost identically to Mirza Baba, but without the decoration on his chest. In addition, a document, written in Persian, is stuffed into his *kamarband*, rather than a dagger. According to Idesbald, Mirza Mas'ud was about 50 years old and had a sympathetic countenance and an air of intelligence. He spoke French well, read Voltaire, subscribed to French newspapers which were sent to him at Tabriz from Tblisi, and was, in short, a man of the world such as one might meet in Paris, Vienna or London.[153]

MAR YOHANNA

Mar Yohanna[154] was a native of Gol'adhan,[155] a village on the Salmas plain,[156] who became a lifelong friend and associate of the American Mission at Urmia beginning in 1831 when he first met the Rev. Eli Smith (1801–57)[157] and his

---

153. Idesbald 1833: 83.

154. His name appears both as Yohanna and Yohannan. Fowler 1858: 459 noted that the Nestorian Syriac form was Yohanna, the Hebrew was Yohannan, and the standard Syriac was Yuhanon. As Perkins 1861: 19 wrote, 'The term Mar is literally *lord*, (dominus,) the same as is used in the gospels and the epistles.'

155. For the transcription of the name I thank my friend and colleague Willem Floor (Bethesda MD). The name appears on modern maps as Golozan. Müller-Simonis 1892: 580, called it 'Gulizan.'

156. 'He is himself from Gooleeza in Salmás....His diocese consists of twelve villages, eight of which are in Oormiah, and the rest in Térgaver, a mountainous district just back of Jamálava to the west. In this village there is no school, nor can any read, except himself, his father and two brothers.' See Smith 1833: 220. During his travels through this area W.F. Ainsworth 'stopped in the gardens of the Chaldean village of Gawalán [Gavlan], to the N. of which is a larger Christian village called Jemalawah by the Chaldean residents, but Jelálábád by the Persians.' See Ainsworth 1841: 60.

157. A native of Northland, CT, Smith was an 1821 graduate of Yale and an 1826 graduate of the Andover Theological Seminary. Expecting originally to work at the ABCFM.'s printing press on Malta, Smith studied Arabic in Cairo with the Swiss cleric Rev. Samuel Gobat (1799–1879), a former pupil of the renowned Parisian Orientalist Antoine Isaac Silvestre de Sacy (1758–1838). In 1835 Smith conducted an exploratory survey of Palestine and the Sinai peninsula with Edward Robinson (1794-1863). Thereafter he went to Leipzig where he supervised the manufacture of a font for printing Arabic. As Franklin Bowditch Dexter noted in 1913, 'He had collected the best models of Arabic calligraphy from Cairo, Damascus, Aleppo, and Constantinople, and had spent many months of intense application in drawing from them the diagrams from which the punches for the matrices were cut. The result was "the most beautiful font of Arabic type the world had ever seen," which soon became, and has since remained, the standard for Arabic print.' See Dexter 1913: 81. Cf. Anonymous 1833: 139; Anderson 1872: 322; Carter 1918: 18. Sarah Lanman Huntington Smith, Eli Smith's wife, came from Norwich, CT, and was largely responsible for the success of the first school for girls in the Ottoman Empire which had been founded at Beirut in 1833 by Eliza N. Hanna Thomson (1800-1834) and Martha W. Merrill Dodge (1810-1886). See Hooker 1839: 381–90; Laurie 1864: 23.

colleague, the Rev. Harrison Gray Otis Dwight (1803–62),[158] during their exploratory reconnaissance of missionizing needs in Turkey, Armenia, Georgia and
western Iran on behalf of the American Board of Commissioners of Foreign
Missions.[159] On 21 September, 1833, the Rev. Justin Perkins (1805–69)[160] and
his wife, Charlotte Bass Perkins (1808–97),[161] set sail from Boston in the brig
George, Capt. Hallet, bound for Constantinople via Malta. From there they
travelled by sea to Trabzon on the Black Sea, proceeding overland via Erzurum
to Tabriz and Urmia where they established the American Mission. In 1841, on
account of his wife's poor health, Justin and Charlotte Perkins decided to visit
the United States.[162] Since Perkins corresponded regularly with both friends
and Christian periodicals in New England, the American public learned, in
December, 1841, that the Perkins family was accompanied on their journey by
Mar Yohanna. In the United States Perkins and Mar Yohanna travelled for nine
months together, attending services at innumerable churches as well as meetings
of religious societies. Mar Yohanna even went to the White House — the first
Persian to do so — where he met President John Tyler.[163]

Mar Yohanna's travels were well-documented in the press up and down the
eastern seaboard of the United States and there is no question that the Bishop
became an object of fascination. As one writer observed, Mar Yohanna, 'with

---

158. A native of Conway, MA, Dwight was an 1825 graduate of Hamilton College. From
     there he proceeded to Andover Theological Seminary from which he graduated in 1828.
     For over 30 years Dwight worked among the large Armenian community in Constantinople.
     See Anonymous 1862: 96; Anderson 1872: 96; Dwight 1871: 404.

159. Hereafter ABCFM. See Smith 1833; Leavy 1992.

160. A native of West Springfield, MA, Perkins was an 1829 graduate of Amherst and an
     1832 graduate of the Andover Theological Seminary, where he also worked as a tutor
     during the academic year 1832–3. See Anonymous 1908: 133. Apart from his 1841–1843
     visit to America, Perkins labored at Urmia almost non-stop for thirty-five years (1834
     –1869) and wrote extensively about his experiences. See e.g. Perkins 1861.

161. Charlotte Bass came from Middlebury, VT and was married to Justin Perkins on 21
     July 1833, just a month after his ordination and two months before sailing to Constanti-
     nople. Her career as a teacher and missionary at Urmia spanned 24 years, from 1833 to
     1857. See Perkins 1887: 11.

162. Perkins wrote from Constantinople on 14 September announcing their journey. See
     'Monthly Concert, in Park-street Church, Boston — Dec. 6,' *Boston Recorder* (Boston
     MA), December 10, 1841.

163. Mar Yohanna, the Nestorian Bishop,' *Salem Register* (Salem MA), May 9, 1842.

his heavy black beard and *mustaches* presents a singular and interesting appearance.'[164] Another commented on 'his dark, brilliant eyes, and oriental features, with his black and flowing beard.'[165] One wrote of Mar Yohanna's '*majestic beard* — long, glossy and black.'[166] Some called his complexion 'darker, it is said, than that of his countrymen in general,'[167] while others described it as 'somewhat between a dark olive, and a slight tinge of yellow.'[168] With 'eyes and other features finely formed,'[169] 'his hair and beard, the latter worn at length after the eastern style, of jet black,'[170] the figure of Mar Yohanna 'altogether makes a very commanding appearance.'[171] In short, he was 'a fine dignified person, the ample and commanding expression of which,'[172] was enhanced by his attire.

According to one observer, Mar Yohanna's 'flowing robes, ample turban, and serious air, gave him an unusually grave and venerable aspect.'[173] As another noted, 'His dress — the flowing Persian robes, is described as fantastic and picturesque, rather than elegant or graceful. — His turban was formed of a large shawl twined round his head — to which was appended behind a large tail of red cloth.'[174] When Mar Yohanna appeared in church or at a public gathering, 'having taken off his large red turban, which he wore on his head,' he was 'dressed in

---

164. 'Arrival of Mr. Perkins and Mar Yohanna,' *Boston Recorder* (Boston MA), 21 January 21, 1842; 'Arrival of Mr. Perkins and Mar Yohanna,' *Christian Reflector* (Worcester MA), 26 January 26, 1842.

165. '[Correspondence of the Christian Observer.] New York, May 12th. American Tract Society,' *Christian Observer* (Philadelphia PA), May 20, 1842.

166. 'The Nestorian Bishop, Mar Yohannan, *Oswego Palladium* (Oswego NY), May 25, 1842.

167. 'Mar Yohanna at Washington,' *Christian Observer* (Philadelphia PA), May 6, 1842; 'Mar Yohanna at Washington,' *The Ohio Observer* (Hudson OH), May 26, 1842.

168. 'Mar Yohanna — A Nestorian Bishop,' *Bay State Democrat* (Boston MA), February 28, 1842; 'Mar Yohanna — A Nestorian Bishop,' *New-York Evening Post* (New York NY), March 1, 1842; 'Mar Yohanna — A Nestorian Bishop,' *Republican Farmer* (Bridgeport CT), March 8, 1842.

169. 'The Nestorian Bishop, Mar Yohannan,' *Oswego Palladium*.

170. 'Mar Yohanna — A Nestorian Bishop,' *Bay State Democrat*; 'Mar Yohanna — A Nestorian Bishop,' *New-York Evening Post*; 'Mar Yohanna — A Nestorian Bishop,' *Republican Farmer*.

171. 'Untitled,' *The Jamestown Journal* (Jamestown NY), April 14, 1842.

172. 'Mar Yohanna at Washington,' *Christian Observer*; 'Mar Yohanna at Washington,' *The Ohio Observer*.

173. 'Evening Session,' *New-York Evangelist* (New York NY), January 27, 1842.

174. 'The Nestorian Bishop, Mar Yohannan,' *Oswego Palladium*.

the costume of his country, wearing a loose garment over and around his person coming down to his ancles [sic].'[175] Another commentator noted, 'He appeared in the garb of his native country, but as he wore a cloak it was difficult to see precisely the fashion of his dress. His pantaloons, however, appeared to be very full, and his dress above the waist very tight.— There was much red about the whole, and the bottom of his pants appeared to be entirely so.'[176]

The exotic appearance of the bishop from Iran that made such an impression on audiences and congregations up and down the eastern seaboard was memorialized on three occasions. From news reports it is clear that Perkins and Mar Yohanna visited Boston in late February, 1842. While there, Mar Yohanna had his portrait painted by Charles Hubbard (1801-1875) in his Tremont Row studio. Little is known of Hubbard's artistic career. Born in Brighton, Massachusetts, Hubbard worked as a boy in the construction of the fortifications of Boston during the War of 1812[177] and served as a captain in the 2nd Massachusetts Regiment from 1829 to 1831.[178] Although he was eventually considered 'an artist of some little fame' who 'earned a modest fortune by his painting,'[179] it is clear that he was primarily a commercial artist. An advertisement for C. Hubbard, 8 State Street, Military Standard and Sign Painting, published in the *Boston Annual Advertiser* and dated July 5, 1823, announced to the public that 'he will be happy to execute orders in the following branches of his professions — viz. Military Standard Paintings, Plain and Ornamental Sign Do., Masonic and Fancy Do., Landscape and Marine Do., Clock and Timepiece Dial Do., Gilt and Painted Ornaments for ships, done at short notice, Coach and Chaise Bodies Ornamented with Arms, Initials, Borders, &c. Transparencies for Window Curtains, painted with Elegant Views, Drawings for Models, Machinery, &c. and Designs and Drawings for Cards, Diplomas, &c.'[180] A volunteer militia snare drum, painted

---

175. 'Proceedings of Wednesday Evening. Rev. Mr. Perkins' Address,' *Christian Observer* (Philadelphia PA), January 28, 1842.

176. 'Untitled,' *The Jamestown Journal*.

177. Munsell 1899: 209.

178. Mackenzie 1917: 266.

179. Day 1895: 428.

180. Anonymous 1823: full page advertisement unpaginated.

by Hubbard in 1824 for the Boston City Guards, is an example of this work.[181] Similarly, Stimpson's *Boston Directory* of 1832 contains an advertisement for 'Charles Hubbard, Sign, Block, Ornamental, Military Standard and Masonic Painter,'[182] and Hubbard was still advertising his services 'as a sign and ornamental painter, and painter of military standards and masonic regalia'[183] in 1834. By 1837, however, Hubbard appears to have turned his hand to portraiture. That year he exhibited two portraits at the First Exhibition and Fair of the Massachusetts Charitable Mechanic Association,[184] and for the rest of his life he listed himself in a succession of Boston commercial directories as a portrait painter.[185] Moreover, Hubbard's painting of his own family at home, dating to 1841,[186] shows what he was capable of around the time that he did Mar Yohanna's portrait. Nevertheless, it is also a fact that Hubbard served as a Director of the Winnesinimet Ferry Company[187] and the New England Mutual Life Insurance Company, suggesting he could not rely on his painting to support himself and his family. Hubbard also served as a Selectman representing Chelsea and was in the state senate for two terms, beginning in 1851 and 1852.[188] It is likely that his political and business activities diminished the amount of time he devoted to portraiture over the years.

---

181. Guthman 1982: 155, Fig. 12. A second drum, possibly the work of Hubbard, is in the Museum of Fine Arts, Boston (Accession Number 2015.2925; H: 20", Dia.: 17", maple and calfskin).

182. Anonymous 1832: 6.

183. Groce and Wallace 1957: s.v. Hubbard, Charles (1801-1876).

184. Anonymous 1837: 31, 'Water-colored Drawing. Well drawn;' 32, 'Two Portraits;' and 84, 'The Lancers' Standard — a fine work of art of the kind, leaving nothing to be desired, though the costume of the Indian on the reverse may be somewhat too fanciful. The Standard for the N. England Guards is also very good.'

185. See e.g Anonymous 1841: 77; Anonymous 1844: 132; Anonymous 1847: 93; Anonymous 1850: 196; Anonymous 1852: 134; Anonymous 1855: 159; Anonymous 1859: 469; Anonymous 1866b: 536.

186. 'Charles Hubbard and His Family,' oil on wood, 1840-1841. H: 10 7/8", W: 14". Collection of the Shelburne Museum, museum purchase, acquired from Maxim Karolik. 1959-265.26. Shelburne VT. For this painting as an illustration of New England domesticity see Nylander 1994: 255.

187. Founded in 1631, the Winnisimmet Ferry linked Boston, Charlestown and Chelsea, the original name of which was Winnisimmet. It was the oldest ferry in New England and probably in North America. See Chamberlain 1908: 85.

188. Munsell 1899: 209; Molyneux 1904: 85; Mackenzie 1917: 266.

Fig. 27. The whereabouts of Charles Hubbard's original portrait of Mar Yohanna are unknown. That this is a faithful rendition of it, however, is virtually guaranteed by the reputation of its engraver, Jarvis Griggs Kellogg. Mar Yohanna, a clergyman, is dressed modestly but not without some decoration in his patterned turban and kamarband. His gaze is directed squarely at the viewer and his facial features and beard suggest that this is a realistic portrait without any attempt to embellish or stylize the sitter's appearance.

Although the whereabouts of Hubbard's painted portrait are unknown,[189] an engraving of it, by Jarvis Griggs Kellogg (1805-1873),[190] who had trained in Boston with Oliver Pelton (1798-1882),[191] appeared in 1843 as one of the 'Embellishments,' actually the Frontispiece, of *The Christian Souvenir* (Fig. 27). The volume also contained a chapter entitled, 'Mar Yohannan,' by the Rev. D. Crosby.[192] This is less a biographical study of the bishop than a *précis* for American readers of the history of the Nestorian or Assyrian Church of the East.[193]

As one anonymous writer noted, during his stay in America, Mar Yohanna 'wore the dress of his own people, and the long black beard that fell upon his

---

189. It appears in Lane and Browne 1906: 1592.

190. Jarvis Griggs Kellogg was the elder brother of the better known Daniel Wright Kellogg (1807-1874) who founded the hugely successful lithography house of D.W. Kellogg & Co. at Hartford, Connecticut, in 1833. See Carey 1954: 90. For his career see Brashears 2009: 120. Two other brothers, Edmund Burke Kellogg (1809-1872) and Elijah Chapman Kellogg (1811-1881), were also engravers. For a retrospective exhibition of their work see Anonymous 1952.

191. O'Brien 2003: 5.

192. Crosby 1843. The author was almost certainly the Rev. Daniel Crosby (1799-1843), an 1823 Yale graduate who completed his theological studies in 1826 at Andover Theological Seminary. He was the first rector of Winthrop Church in Charlestown, Massachusetts, where he was installed on 14 August, 1833. In May, 1842, he commenced editorial work for the ABCFM at Mission House in Boston, but died in Charlestown on 28 February, 1843. At the time of Mar Yohanna's visit, in 1842, he was Assistant Recording Secretary of the ABCFM. See Packard 1854: 106; Anderson 1862: 411. For Crosby's life see Greene 1843.

193. As Brock 1996: 28-29 noted, 'Just as in politics today a right-wing politician might try to smear his socialist opponent by calling him a communist, so in the religious polemics of the fifth and sixth centuries one side would try to put the other side into disrepute by calling it by the name of someone, or some party, that had already been publically condemned as heretical. Since Nestorius had been condemned at the Council of Ephesus in 431, "Nestorian" was a convenient dirty word with which to tar any of one's theological opponents who followed the Antiochene christological tradition.' Nevertheless, the term Nestorian will be retained here simply because that is the way the group was invariably referred to in the 19th century sources cited below.

breast gave him a peculiarly venerable and remarkable appearance.'[194] The Hubbard-Kellogg portrait of Mar Yohanna gives every appearance of being highly realistic, drawn from life without attempting to idealize the sitter. It shows the bishop sporting a large, black beard. We see just a hint of his white shirt (*pirahan*); capacious, striped and patterned turban (*'amameh, delband*);[195] and a jacket (*arkhaliq*)[196] belted with a shawl (*kamarband*)[197] around his waist, a portion of which loops up around his left shoulder, hanging down over his right side. His shoulders are somewhat rounded and his face is heavy, giving a distinct feeling of weight and mass to the portrait. His eyes stare straight at the viewer. His eyebrows, eyes, nose, lips and left ear are all realistically depicted, without any hint of stylization. A dark cloak (*qaba*)[198] is gathered about Mar Yohanna's torso. In fact, the Hubbard-Kellogg portrait of Mar Yohanna may be compared favorably with one journalist's description of him on the occasion when he received communion from Bishop Albert Viets Griswold (1766-1843) at Grace Church, probably just shortly before Hubbard painted his portrait:

---

194. Anonymous 1848: 139. The singularity of Mar Yohanna's beard was commented upon by Perkins who noted that, during his 1842 trip to America, he 'saw not a single beard except that on the face of Mar Yohannan. On reaching Boston, at the close of 1858, one of the wonders that surprised me was a beard on at least every third man of all professions. Little did I anticipate that the venerable appendages then beginning to drop from the chins of those staid Orientals were so suddenly to migrate and reappear on the youthful and the aged faces of so many of my countrymen.' See Perkins 1861: 86, n. *.

195. According to Floor 1999b: 249, in the Qajar period, 'Members of the religious class… wanted to create the impression that a big turban hid big brains and much intelligence. The more important an *'alem* was the bigger his turban, so much so that the heavy turban would slide from left to right when the wearer was walking.' As Polak 1865: 140 noted, "In früherer Zeit war der Turban (amāmeh, dilbænd) die allgemeine Tract; seine Faltung, Größe, Form, Farbe, der überragende oder eingeschlagene Zipfel machte die Bewohner der verschiedenen Länder und Bezirke kenntlich. Jetzt tragen ihn nur noch einige Volk-stämme, die Kurden, Afghanen, Beludschen, und von gewissen Ständen, den Seiiden, Priestern, Schullehrern, Aerzten, Droguisten u.s.w., ward er als Abzeichen beibehalten.' The Kurdish term for the turban is *pač*. See Mohseni and Andrews 1992/2011.

196. Floor 1999b: 252-253.

197. Floor 1999b: 262-264. Polak 1865: 146 wrote that, 'Mittels eines Gürtels (kæmerbænd) wird der Käba zusammengehalten. Der Gürtel besteht aus einem langen mehrmals um den Leib gewundenen Streifen, dessen Ende eingestülpt wird. Die Reichern umgürten sich mit einem Kaschmirshawl.'

198. Floor 1999b: 253-255. As Polak 1865: 145 noted, 'er ist fast immer einfarbig.'

The costume appeared to be a vest fitting tight to the body, as far as the hips, thence descending loosely below the knees; and under this we should judge he wore a pair of loose drawers, or very wide trowsers. Surmounting all was a dark long robe reaching nearly to the feet. In the street he may be occasionally seen with a warm cloth cap, some ten or eleven inches high, and of rather a conical form, which is also worn in the hottest weather, and so fashioned as to rise into four corners at the top.[199]

The only difference between the description and the portrait would seem to be in the omission of the 'warm cloth cap' which Mar Yohanna presumably removed for his indoor sitting.

A second portrait of Mar Yohanna (Fig. 28) was executed in Washington DC by the noted portraitist and lithographer Charles Fenderich (1805-1889).[200] Born Carolus Fendrich in Laufenburg, Canton of Aargau, Switzerland,[201] Fenderich worked in Switzerland and France as a draftsman and lithographer until 1831 when he emigrated with his mother and sister to the United States.[202] After enjoying initial success in Philadelphia Fenderich moved to Washington. By 1837 he had established his Lithographic Repository on Pennsylvania Avenue and begun selling portraits of American presidents, senators and other senior government officials. The series of portraits of statesmen, issued by Charles Fenderich & Co. between 1837 and 1841,[203] was the principal source of the artist's lasting fame,[204] although he is also known for lithographs depicting incidents in the Mexican War (1846-48). The last forty years of Fenderich's life (1849–89) were spent in California, first at Eliza City,[205] and later in San Francisco where he continued

---

199. 'Mar Yohanna — A Nestorian Bishop,' *Bay State Democrat;* 'Mar Yohanna — A Nestorian Bishop,' *New-York Evening Post*; and 'Mar Yohanna — A Nestorian Bishop,' *Republican Farmer*.

200. Parker and Kaplan 1959: 56, no. 221.

201. The surname is spelled variously in contemporary records and appears as Fähndrich, Faehndrich, Faenderich, Fändrich, Fehndrich, Fenderich and Fendrich. Lienhard 1898: 296 referred to him as, 'Ein Schweizer Lithograph, Herr Fähndrich von Laufenburg, Kanton Aargau.'

202. Parker and Kaplan 1959: 3.

203. Weitenkampf 1912: 188.

204. A measure of their popularity is indicated by the fact that these were not just sold in their own right but were also copied by other printers. See Carey 1954: 263–4.

205. He was a shareholder in the newly founded if short-lived community of Eliza City, named after Miss Eliza Sutter, in Yuba County, California. See Lienhard 1898: 296.

to produce portraits of notable citizens of the day. Politically, Fenderich was a liberal. This is perhaps best shown by the fact that, in 1843, at a meeting held in Washington DC, he was named president of a committee organized to raise funds in aid of the Austrian jurist Sylvester Jordan (1792–1861) who had been unlawfully arrested and imprisoned by Hessian authorities in Marburg.[206]

An inscription on Mar Yohanna's portrait tells us that it was dedicated to the ABCFM by the Missionary Societies of the Fourth Presbyterian Church in Washington DC who presumably commissioned and paid for it. The portrait, although drawn by Fenderich, was printed by his colleague Pierre-Étienne (Peter Stephen) Duval (c. 1804/5-1886),[207] in Philadelphia. Both hand-colored and greytone versions of the chine collé print survive. The image of Mar Yohanna is a 'head-and-shoulders portrait, facing slightly left.'[208] The size of the edition is unknown.

The Hubbard-Kellogg and Fenderich portraits differ from each other in a number of important respects. Whereas Mar Yohanna stared straight at his portraitist in the Hubbard-Kellogg image, he gazes off to his right in Fenderich's depiction. While the hands and arms (apart from the left shoulder) of Hubbard-Kellogg's Mar Yohanna cannot be seen, Fenderich had Mar Yohanna sit with his right hand, forefinger and thumb extended, spread across his chest in a somewhat theatrical gesture. This is a variant of the well-documented, hand-over-the-heart gesture widely attested in Renaissance, Mannerist, Baroque and later art, the interpretation of which has been much discussed by art historians. Some scholars view the gesture as a sign of 'grace, elegance and refinement.'[209] Others have suggested it is a representation of 'laying the hand on the breast whilst inciting one's inner self to grief,' a gesture recommended as a spiritual exercise by the founder of the Jesuit Order, Saint Ignatius of Loyola, or an illustration of 'the

---

206. Wust 1959: 41.

207. A French émigré considered the greatest of Philadelphia's lithographers. See Leatherwax 2012: 97. For his own exposition of lithography see Duval 1871. Duval's authorship of this entry is credited by the editor on p. viii of the volume. Duval exerted great influence and his expertise was widely appreciated, witness the fact that he began producing color lithographs in 1849 for which he won a bronze medal at the World's Fair in London in 1850. See e.g. Reps 1984: 29, 35. As Todd 1939: 167 noted, 'He had come to this country from France in 1831 to manage a new lithographic department which had been opened in the engraving firm of Cephas Grosvenor Childs (1793-1871), and later he took over Child's business. In many respects Duval was a pioneer in the industry.'

208. Library of Congress. https://www.loc.gov/item/2017657788.

209. Lazzeri, Nicoli and Zhang 2019: 532.

From Life on Stone by

Ch⁵ Fenderich
1842

Fig. 28. Charles Fenderich's colorful, lithographic portrait of Mar Yohanna presents him in a modest, yet dignified pose, dressed in two tones of blue, with floral patterns adorning both his turban and kamarband. In contrast to the Hubbard portrait, the facial features and beard here appear stylized, recalling a European conception of what a Biblical patriarch may have looked like. Fenderich's portraits of American presidents were very popular. Although Mar Yohanna's travels were well-documented in the press, it is unclear how widely disseminated this lithograph may have been.

hand placed on the chest as a sign of moral pain in sinners who were in the act of committing a sin.'[210] James Hall proposed that the 'right hand placed on the left breast' is a gesture of obedience echoing 'Adam at his creation.'[211] Alternatively, following David Morgan, it could be interpreted as a gesture of 'visual piety' or *Schaufrömmigkeit*, embodying 'the eighteenth- and nineteenth-century site of moral control and the public presentation of a sanctified self.'[212]

On his head Mar Yohanna wears a multi-colored, floral-patterned shawl as a turban, on top of which a large, crimson cap with a thick, blue tassel attached, hangs down. This red cap was described in 1833 by the Rev. Eli Smith who noted,

> None of the Nestorian clergy were distinguished from the laity
> by their dress, except the bishops. They wore a Kürdish costume,
> which consisted of a large red cap, hanging down behind and wound
> around with a turban,[213] instead of the conical sheepskin cap of the
> Persians, and of flowing robes somewhat in the Osmanly fashion.

Around his waist Mar Yohanna wore a second, floral-patterned shawl as a *kamarband* or sash.[214] As for his clothing, Mar Yohanna is shown wearing a long-sleeved, white (cotton or linen) shirt,[215] the right arm of which protrudes just slightly at the right wrist. A white shirt was said by Badger to have been typical

---

210. Lazzeri, Nicoli and Zhang 2019: 530.

211. Hall 2018: 122.

212. Morgan 1998: 59.

213. The red cap appears to hang over and off the back of Mar Yohanna's turban, exactly as it does in the portraits of two other Nestorian bishops, Mar Elias and Mar Gabriel. In his description of Kurdish dress, Fraser 1840: 86, mentioned the turban consisting of a large silk shawl 'wound in the most graceful manner;' but the 'ample vest and gown, with magnificent wide Turkish sleeves, over which is worn a jacket, often richly embroidered and furred, according to the owner's rank,' and 'Around their waist, instead of a shawl…a girdle fastened with monstrous silver clasps,' are very different than the dress of Nestorian bishops.

214. Ker Porter 1821: 324, described visiting Fath 'Ali Shah and some of his sons, including 'Abbas Mirza, who wore 'shawl-girdles.' This 'cotton sash' is called a *peštand* in Kurdish. See Mohseni and Andrews 1992/2011.

215. Known in Kurdish as a *kerās*. See Mohseni and Andrews 1992/2011.

of the Nestorians.[216] Over this shirt Mar Yohanna is shown wearing a pale blue, long-sleeved garment, with a patterned border, and a darker blue outer robe, the border of which matches that of his jacket, which probably reached his ankles.[217]

Given Mar Yohanna's colored dress and floral-patterned shawls, one might suppose that he was dressed in finer clothes than most Nestorian bishops would have been at home, but this was not the case, as two colorful illustrations in Justin Perkins' 1843 account of his first eight years in Persia confirm.[218] These show two Nestorian bishops, Mar Elias,[219] the 'aged bishop resident' of Geog (Gug/Gog) Tappeh, a village c. 9 kms. southeast of Urmia, and Mar Gabriel,[220] a younger man about 30 years old, whose village Ardishai lies c. 22 kms. southeast of Urmia. Thayer also made a grey-tone copy of Fenderich's portrait of Mar Yohanna for the book.[221] The portraits of Mar Elias and Mar Gabriel are particularly helpful in clarifying Mar Yohanna's dress for, although differing in coloration, all three men were shown wearing an identical costume. Each has a turban with the floppy red cap, resembling a Scottish tam bonnet, posed on top of it, terminating in

---

216. Badger 1852: 215, wrote, 'The male costume of the Nestorians consists of a wide pair of shalwar, or trowsers, bound round the waist by a running string, or fastened with a girdle, which also secures the end of a vest. Under these is a white cotton shirt, and above a coarse woollen coat, striped with white and black, and reaching to the loins. A conical felt cap, resembling in shape that worn by the Chinese, forms the common head-dress. Priests, however, and the more respectable laymen among them, wear a round cap of the same material, which is secured to the head by a small turban.' This is in fact the way Priest Sadok, brother of the Nestorian patriarch, dressed. See Perkins 1861: 262–3. The full-length portraits of Mar Elias and Mar Gabriel confirm, however, that the Nestorian bishops closer to Urmia did not wear *shalwar*.

217. For the conventions of Qajar-period dress see Diba 2011.

218. In the preface of his book Perkins noted that, 'The colored plates were originally drawn by a Persian artist, under my supervision.' See Perkins 1861: viii. After his return to the United States, Perkins turned these drawings over to B.W. Thayer & Co., a lithography establishment in Boston active in the early and mid-1840s, who prepared the illustrations for Perkins' book. Benjamin W. Thayer's (1814-1875) lithography business, at 204 Washington St., operated from 1840 to 1847, and again from 1851 to 1853. See Pierce and Slautterback 1991: 130.

219. Perkins 1861: between pp. 234 and 235. Not to be confused with the Patriarch of the same name.

220. Perkins 1861: between pp. 272 and 273.

221. Perkins 1861: between pp. 172 and 173. It is unclear why he did not or could not use Fenderich's lithograph itself but this presumably related to a copyright issue for Perkins must have supplied Thayer with the print from which he worked in copying Mar Yohanna's portrait.

a blue tassel. The use of colored material for the turbans of Nestorian bishops was confirmed by Perkins when he described a visit, early in his stay at Urmia, to the Patriarch Elias. 'His dress resembled that of the bishops,' Perkins wrote, 'except that the shawl of his turban is black, while theirs are of several colors.'[222]

Mar Yohanna, Mar Elias and Mar Gabriel are all shown wearing a long-sleeved, long gown, with trim or piping (black in the case of Mar Elias and Mar Gabriel, patterned in Mar Yohanna's case). The cuff of Mar Elias' right sleeve shows a triangular projection known in Kurdish as a *sorāni*,[223] a hint of which can also be detected on Mar Yohanna's wrist in Fenderich's portrait. Their gowns were belted at the waist with a shawl *kamarband* or *peštand*. The images of Mar Elias and Mar Gabriel show that this gown reached the ankles. An outer, sleeved-cloak completed the costume. This could be worn with the arms in the sleeves, as Mar Yohanna did when he sat for Fenderich's portrait, or with the arms protruding from slits in the side and the sleeves left to hang down. Mar Elias is shown with his right arm protruding from inside the cloak, the right sleeve hanging down; and the left arm protruding through the slit, again with the left sleeve shown hanging empty. In Mar Gabriel's case we see his right arm protruding through a slit in the cloak. His left arm is not shown. Perkins noted that, 'Mar Yohannan's cloak is *the common Persian cloak*, worn alike by all sects and classes in Persia…nothing but the bishop's CAP, in his dress, being peculiar and distinctive of his *clerical* office.'[224]

Mar Yohanna is depicted in both portraits with a full beard, yet the Hubbard-Kellogg rendering appears far more lifelike, whereas Fenderich's version of Mar Yohanna's beard and straight nose gives him the look of an idealized historical figure, more of a Henry Wadsworth Longfellow or Walt Whitman than a 19th century Persian. In the absence of any photographs of Mar Yohanna, how is one to decide whether Hubbard-Kellogg or Fenderich is the more faithful portrait? Unexpectedly the answer is provided by an image in an altogether different medium, the silhouette.

In late August 1842, Perkins and Mar Yohanna were in Upstate New York, where they visited Niagara Falls, Buffalo and the Auburn Theological Seminary.[225]

---

222. Perkins 1861: 180.

223. Mohseni and Andrews 1992/2011.

224. Perkins 1861: 360.

225. See 'Items of News and Items of Choice,' *The Daily Chronicle* (Philadelphia PA), August 20, 1842; 'Correspondence Commercial Advertiser. Auburn, August 17, 1842. Auburn Theological Seminary,' *New-York Spectator* (New York NY), August 31, 1842.

By 1857 Auburn had become an important stop on the Underground Railroad, conveying escaped slaves to Canada.[226] A year later the former Governor of New York and then Senator, William Henry Seward (1801-1872), sold 'a little patch of ground with a house on it, at Auburn, near his own home,'[227] to the former slave and legendary abolitionist, Harriet Tubman where, after the Civil War, she and her parents lived. In 1842, however, Auburn was a very different place. It was still recovering from the financial collapse of 1837 that had devastated the local economy of this small, Upstate New York town. Indeed, its population in 1845 was only 6,171.[228] Nevertheless, Auburn boasted a Theological Seminary, founded in 1820 by the Presbyterian Synod,[229] and this, combined with the town's location on the way to Buffalo and Niagara Falls, was probably the main reason that Perkins and Mar Yohanna stopped there.

After their travels in western New York, presumably *en route* for Albany where they were on 11 September, Perkins and Mar Yohanna made a stop at the well-known spa town, Saratoga Springs, about 40 miles north of the state capital. A guidebook from 1845 called Saratoga Springs somewhat hyperbolically

> probably the most celebrated watering place on the Globe; strangers from about every part of the world annually congregate here during the Summer months…thus giving the otherwise quiet village all the appearance, as far as population is concerned, of a large city.[230]

---

226. Still 1872: 54, 104, 323, 517.

227. Bradford 1869: 80. Although originally a native of Florida, Orange County, New York, Seward had moved to Auburn in 1822 when, after passing the bar exam, he joined a law firm there. See Seward 1891: 51. In 1868, as Secretary of State, Seward secured a pension for Tubman in recognition of 'services rendered in the Union Army during the late war.' See Bradford 1869: 64.

228. Hall 1869: 260.

229. As Hall 1869: 373–4 observed, 'A vast army of emigrants was daily landing on the shores and pouring across the States toward the far west, where villages and new States were being called into existence as if by magic…Few divines, however, came out into the new country except as missionaries…Many a pulpit already established was vacant, and there were none to fill them. The graduates of the Seminaries were generally detained in the Eastern States. The Presbyterian Church viewed the state of things in Western New York with some anxiety. Here was a wide field for religious work, but the laborers therein were few.'

230. Anonymous 1845: 162–3.

Fig. 29. When it comes to portraiture any limitations of the silhouette genre are certainly compensated for by the extraordinary artistry of Auguste Edouart. This double portrait of Justin Perkins and Mar Yohanna, showing both in full figure, captures innumerable details that convey a realistic impression of them. Mar Yohanna's eyelash, his nose (so like that seen in Hubbard's portrait, Fig. 27), the overhanging moustache, the wisps of hair at the bottom of his beard, the long tassel suspended from his cap, and the gesture of his raised hand, combine to give the impression of a living being in conversation with his missionary colleague on whom the viewer has suddenly stumbled.

As Andrew Oliver noted in 1977, 'What a social lion the bishop of Ooroomiah, Mar Yohannan, must have been at Saratoga that August.'[231] Although not mentioned in the news coverage of their travels, the presence of Perkins and Mar Yohanna in Saratoga Springs is confirmed by silhouettes of both men cut on 27 August 27, 1842, by the famed French silhouette artist, Auguste (Augustin Amant Fidèle) Edouart (1789-1861) (Fig. 29).[232] As Edith Stanwood Bolton noted in 1915, 'Edouart visited every large city in the United States during the ten years he spent here,[233] but he did a vast deal at Saratoga in 1841 and 1842.'[234] It was his practice 'to take up his abode in a town, to advertise in the papers, and to stay there while he took the silhouette portraits of the surrounding gentry and noblemen.'[235] According to Sherrill Schell, while there, Edouart 'made his cuttings under a tent. Men and women of fashion sought him out, and the likenesses he made are treasured by many families.'[236] Between 1839 and 1849,[237] while working in the United States, Edouart cut over 50,000 silhouette portraits, some 10,000 of which were of children. These were, in the words of the British writer and publisher Andrew White Tuer (1838-1900), 'portraits of numerous somebodies amongst innumerable nobodies.'[238] Duplicates of the silhouettes that he sold, or 'counterparts' as he called them, were carefully kept in fifty large scrap-books.[239]

---

231. Andrew Oliver 1977: 207.

232. Published in Oliver 1977: 207, no. 208.

233. The full extent of his travels is unknown. According to Crawford 1915: 344, he worked in 'New York, Saratoga, Philadelphia, Norwich, and Boston, as well as in many cities of the south.' Nevill Jackson 1921: 188 contains the names of over 300 cities and towns 'visited by Edouart or mentioned in the home address of his sitters.' With respect to his travels, this statement is potentially misleading, particularly as some of the sitters from far-flung states like Louisiana, Kentucky, Indiana, Alabama and Arkansas may have sat for him while visiting New York or Saratoga and not in their home states. Nevertheless, if even a fraction of the names represent the extent of his travels, then he must have covered the greater part of the eastern United States.

234. Bolton 1915: 61.

235. Nevill Jackson 1911: 52.

236. Schell 1923: 39.

237. Nevill Jackson 1921: 191.

238. Tuer 1890: 170.

239. One reason Edouart did this was purely commercial. As he wrote, 'A copy of every Likeness taken, is kept by me, in books for the purpose; so that at any time, the person or friends may have as many duplicates as they require, and at a less price.' See Edouart 1835: 23. According to Béland 1992: 44, Edouart charged 3 shillings per duplicate.

Disaster struck on 21 December, 1849. While returning to France aboard the *Oneida*, Edouart was shipwrecked in Vazon Bay off Guernsey and lost most of his scrap-books. As Tuer noted,

> About a dozen books were fished up from the wreck,[240] but, though carefully sponged and dried, they were almost ruined. The loss of the greater part of his collection so prayed upon the old man's mind that he forsook his profession, presenting, before he left the island, what remained of his silhouettes to Mrs. Lukis…in grateful recognition of many kindnesses.[241]

Twenty years later, in 1911, the silhouette historian Emily (Mrs. Frederick) Nevill Jackson (1861-1947) advertised in *The Connoisseur* for any information on the whereabouts of the surviving Edouart scrap-books and the grandson of Frederica Lukis came forward and sold her the scrap-books. Jackson published a catalogue of the collection[242] before selling 3712 of them, apparently the bulk of the American silhouettes, to Arthur Stannard Vernay who catalogued and exhibited them in New York between 27 October and 15 November, 1913.[243] In 1914 Vernay noted, 'His American portraits which I recently acquired and which have been on exhibition in New York, show how excellently Edouart posed his subjects….As a silhouettist he stands supreme.'[244]

In his *Treatise on Silhouette Likenesses*, written before his arrival in the United States, Edouart made some striking points concerning the accuracy of silhouettes and the insufficiencies of portraiture which help put the work of lesser artists that was available to the broader population, as opposed to that of true masters, in perspective. He wrote,

---

240. The exact number is unclear. According to Oliver 1977: vii, sixteen albums survived, ten of which were of English sitters and six of Americans. Each contained 300 silhouettes. Cf. Anonymous 1913: Karel 1992: 281. Included among the surviving American silhouettes were counterparts of both Mar Yohanna and Justin Perkins, as Nevill Jackson 1921: 218, 231 attested in her 'Complete List of 3,600 Silhouette Portraits of American Citizens taken between 1839-1849 by August Edouart during his tour in the United States.' See Nevill Jackson n.d.

241. Cf. Bolton 1915: 61.

242. Nevill Jackson n.d.

243. Vernay 1913: 875; Totten 1916: 261, n. *; Oliver 1970: 213.

244. Vernay 1914: 85.

Many persons start objections against Silhouette Likenesses, and exclaim 'what can you see in them? the eyes, ears, and muscles of the face are lost, and there is merely the forehead, nose, mouth, and chin to be seen.' It is true, that there is little in the profile of the face; but it is equally true, that this little, is quite sufficient to afford a resemblance of the most satisfactory description. It is unreasonable to say, that because merely a few features are represented; a good Likeness cannot be given. There can be no failure, when the execution is accurate....Having only an outline to represent, I have the less work; and the painter, who has to reconcile and harmonize the effects of shadows, runs a greater chance to make an incorrect Likeness than I do. Are there not examples, before our eyes every day; that painters having taken a correct outline, totally lose its effect in finishing the work, when they are blending the lights and shades together. Without doubt there are masters of portrait painting, but those who are good are very few. The difficulties the Artist has to encounter, are beyond description. How many oil and miniature portraits, have cost immense prices, which have not given the least satisfaction. The combination of colors to render the expression, the animation, and physiognomical character, belonging to the person sitting, is another rock, where the best hopes of the painter are commonly wrecked.[245]

Edouart's style was hyper-realistic. As one reviewer wrote, 'he cut out people "as they are", with no nonsense about them.'[246] Bolton observed that, 'He had a great aptitude for seizing the salient point of a face or figure, and in his silhouettes a gesture, a pose, or an arrested movement often gave his portraits a more than photographic likeness.'[247] As Charles Henry Hart noted in 1900, the irony of this statement is that, "The common introduction of the camera put an end to the silhouettists' occupation."[248]

Two of Edouart's subjects, Justin Perkins and Mar Yohanna, while neither gentry nor noblemen, had their likenesses taken and a close examination of the result, from the physiognomy to the stance, displays aspects that neither the Hubbard-Kellogg nor Fenderich portraits come close to capturing. Edouart's silhouette of Mar Yohanna is striking. Despite the fact that it shows us the Nestorian bishop in profile, it is every bit as illustrative as the Hubbard-Kellogg and Fenderich portraits. We see the massive turban and capacious cap, with

---

245. Edouart 1835: 29.

246. B[?]. 1921: 93.

247. Bolton 1915: 62.

248. Hart 1900: 334.

the large tassel hanging down Mar Yohanna's back; his profile, with eyelashes, nose, moustache and long beard; and his bulky figure, far more reminiscent of the Hubbard than the Fenderich portrait. The image is of a large man, even if his outer cloak undoubtedly added greater bulk to his size, vis-à-vis Perkins, who appears quite slender here. That Mar Yohanna was, in fact, a large, even a portly man, is confirmed by an eyewitness who saw him during his brief stay at Saratoga Springs. The American journalist and lawyer, William Leete Stone, Jr. (1835-1906), a longtime resident of the town, although only a boy in 1842, assembled a series of vignettes of life in Saratoga Springs 'from my having been acquainted from boyhood with many octogenarians who have now passed away.'[249] Describing visitors to The Grove, the Saratoga Springs home of the jurist Reuben Hyde Walworth (1788-1867), Stone noted, 'The Grove has known the portly form of Joseph Bonaparte in tights, and the squat figure of Mar Yohannan in multitudinous folds of cloth.'[250] Taken together, Edouart's silhouette and Hubbard's portrait present us with what appears to be a more realistic impression of Mar Yohanna during his American sojourn than the idealized if elegant portrait by Fenderich. The silhouettes of Perkins and Mar Yohanna are also noteworthy for their lithographic backgrounds. As Edouart wrote in 1835, 'I have back grounds adapted to the Silhouette Likenesses, which give great relief, and impart greater interest than if they were standing on nothing (I mean pasted upon white paper only,).'[251] The bulding in the background of the Perkins-Yohanna silhouette has not been identified.[252]

---

249. Stone 1875: 1.

250. Stone 1875: 341.

251. Edouart 1835: 13.

252. The silhouettes of Perkins and Mar Yohanna are mounted against a scene showing a Gothic or Neo-Gothic building in the background. From 1815 onwards, Edouart lived in various cities and towns in England, Scotland and Ireland. It is known that, while in Ireland, the firm of Unkles & Klason, 26 South Mall, Cork, prepared a number of lithographs of interior and exterior architectural scenes for Edouart's backgrounds, as did the draftsman William Murray in Edinburgh. See e.g. Knipe 2002: 2010. As Nevill Jackson 1921: 8 noted, 'In the Treatise published in 1835 the illustrations have quite elaborate backgrounds, either in brushwork or pencil. At first he executed these himself, but later employed men to do it for him…afterwards lithograph interiors were used for mounting the portraits ordered by his clients. Several of these, unused both interiors and outside scenes, were found with his Folios.' The building that served as the backdrop for the silhouettes of Perkins and Mar Yohanna resembles the Collegiate-style Quadrangle of University College Cork, founded in 1845, i.e. after the silhouettes were done. It may simply be a generic collegiate-ecclesiastical building concocted by Unkles & Klason as a suitable background for Edouart to use.

In concluding this discussion it is appropriate to ask, what kind of prices might have been demanded for Mar Yohanna's portraits? What sorts of comparisons are available? In 1806 two 12" x 10" oil portraits by Thomas Sully were sold for $15 and $30, respectively.[253] When Charles Dickens visited America in 1842, precisely the same year as Mar Yohanna did, his portrait was painted by Francis Alexander (1800–1880), considered by contemporaries 'one of our most successful portrait painters.'[254] At the beginning of his career Alexander charged $15 to $25 per portrait, but by 1831, when he went to Italy, he was charging 'forty dollars for the head and shoulders, twenty-five by thirty inch canvas, and more according to the size,' and later $50 and $75 'for the kit-cat size.'[255] After his return to America in 1833 Alexander was able to command $100 per portrait.[256]

---

253. Fabian 1983: 17. By 1822, however, Sully could command $500 for his full-length portrait of Thomas Jefferson. For the sake of comparison, it is interesting to consider the experiences of Samuel F.B. Morse (1791-1872) who, 'condemned to migratory wanderings in New Hampshire in 1816 and 1817…eked out a marginal existence on fifteen-dollar portraits.' See Staiti 1981: 270. Similarly, in 1818, while in Charleston, South Carolina, Morse painted 'portraits at fifteen dollars. See Prime 1875: 109. That Morse was hardly a successful portrait painter should come as no suprise. Indeed, although his mother wrote to him (letter of 19 December, 1814), 'You must not expect to paint anything in this country, for which you receive any money to support you, but portraits,' Morse protested, 'I cannot be happy unless I am pursuing the intellectual branch of the art. Portraits have none of it.' Staiti 1981: 269. Morse's conviction that portraiture did not belong to 'the intellectual branch' of painting is perfectly consistent with what Elliott 2012: 81-82 referred to as portraiture's 'paradoxical high social importance and low aesthetic value' which earned it dubious praise from one critic who wrote, in 1831, 'However inferior a branch of Fine Art portrait-painting may be deemed, it is at least a prominent and important one.'

254. Dunlap 1834: 432.

255. H: 36" x W: 28–29", so-called after Sir Godfrey Kneller's (1646–1723) portraits of all forty-two members of the Kit-Cat Club in London. The Kit-Cat Club originally met at the home of pastry cook Christopher (Kit) Catt in Shire Lane but later meetings were more often held in Down Place at the home of Jacob Tonson (1655-1736), the poet John Dryden's (1631-1700) publisher. 'The club consisted of noblemen and gentlemen, at the head of whom was the Earl of Dorset. It originated as a convivial association about the time of the Revolution; but as the members of it were, generally speaking, of a Whiggish turn of mind, it gradually assumed a political character. Addison, Steel, Walpole, and Marlborough, firm and fast friends of the Hanoverian succession, were amongst its members. It is principally, however, from their portraits that the fame of the reunions of the Club has been handed down to posterity. These were painted by Sir Godfrey Kneller, and were all of one size, viz. 28 inches or 29 inches by 36 inches. This size has since been called the Kit-cat size.' See Lowndes 1870: 406.

256. Dunlap 1834: 432.

Another relevant record of the price paid by a painter who was just starting his career comes from a newspaper report of June 24, 1846. According to a story that first appeared in the Baltimore newspaper, *The Sun*, entitled 'A Chicago painter in London,' the British-born, American painter, Samuel Marsden Brookes (1816–1892),[257] who had emigrated with his family to Chicago in 1833 when he was seventeen years old, and later became moderately well-known for his still lives, particularly those of fish, returned to London in 1845 where he enjoyed some success as a portraitist.

> A Mr. Marsden Brooks, a young artist from Chicago, Ill., is attracting a good deal of attention in London by his paintings. The Comptroller of the city employed him to paint a miniature of himself, giving him $30, which was so striking a likeness, that a Persian Prince requested permission to carry it to Persia, and Mr. Brooks was of course engaged to paint another. Since then several others have been ordered. Thus a painter from a twelve year old city goes to the largest Metropolis of Europe, and executes orders for Asia![258]

Although no records of Hubbard's prices for portraits appear to have survived, on analogy with those charged by Sully, Alexander and Brookes early in their careers, an estimate of $15–30 is probably not too far from the mark.[259]

As for Mar Yohanna's silhouette, in America Edouart seems to have maintained the prices he had previously charged in England, viz. five shillings for full length figures and one shilling for just a head-and-shoulders.[260] This was considered reasonable by some sitters until they discovered that he could produce

---

257. Born at Newington Green, Middlesex, England, Brookes (often written Brooks) and his family moved to Chicago in 1833, and eventually moved to Milwaukee and San Francisco. For his life see Marshall 1957. His portraits of Native American chiefs were acquired by and displayed in the Historical Society of Wisconsin. See e.g. Thwaites 1889, 1892.

258. 'A Chicago painter in London,' *The Sun* (Baltimore MD), June 24, 1846. Reprinted in the *Richmond Whig and Public Advertiser* (Richmond VA), June 26, 1846; *Easton Star* (Easton MD), July 7, 1846; *Wisconsin Democrat* (Madison WI), July 18, 1846; and *The True American* (Lexington KY), September 2, 1846.

259. As Channing 1921: 300 noted, 'Most of the artistic work of that time was in portraiture. Artists travelled from town to town in America, reproducing with more or less faithfulness the lineaments of almost countless men and women. Oftentimes they charged small prices for their services and spent little time at the work; but they perpetuated for us the faces and forms of their generation of American men and women.'

260. Béland 1992: 44.

a likeness in five minutes. As one exclaimed, 'What! a Shilling a minute, are you not ashamed of yourself? at that rate you must soon become rich.' To this Edouart replied, 'But, Sir, of what consequence is the time to you, if I give you a Likeness, which will please your friends, as well as you have been with those in the show-room…you may stop five hours if you choose in the room, and I shall not charge a penny more for it.'[261]

It is also instructive to compare these prices with contemporary charges for a daguerreotype portrait. In 1842 photography was, in much of the United States, not yet an option for those seeking a likeness of themselves. Louis-Jacques Mandé Daguerre's (1787-1851) process was only just being introduced. The American painter and inventor Samuel F.B. Morse spent several days with Daguerre in France in March, 1839, and a letter to Morse's brother, which appeared in the *New-York Observer* on April 20, 1839, gave Americans their first real understanding of the technology.[262] Yet a copy of Daguerre's manual describing the process did not reach the United States until September of that year and it was only in the spring of 1840 that Morse and his partner, the polymath John William Draper (1811-1882), began to take daguerreotype portraits in New York City for the sum of $5. As one writer has noted, 'It seems that the high price initially made the daguerreotype prohibitive for many New Yorkers, for that first summer [1840] at least.'[263] Regardless of whether or not this seemed expensive, the price of a daguerreotype was certainly less than that of a painted portrait.

PERSIAN PORTRAITS AND PORTRAITS OF PERSIANS

This study has, it is hoped, thrown some light on both the Persians who had their portraits painted in the West between the early 17th and the early 19th century, and the remarkably diverse handful of artists in Russia, Austria, France, England and the United States who immortalized them in a variety of media. From miniaturists of the highest caliber, to experimental lithographers, classically-trained masters, engravers, caricaturists and the world's leading silhouettist, the artists who produced the works illustrated here left a remarkable, vibrant record replete with details of dress and ornament characteristic of the higher echelons of Persian

---

261. Edouart 1835: 97.

262. Gillespie 2016: 25.

263. Gillespie 2016: 34. By way of comparison, 1845 prices at the Toledo, Ohio, studio of Robinson & Barney ranged from $1.50 to $3.00. See Gagel 1998: 1. This was still considered expensive, however. As Gagel 1998: 2, noted, "Despite the high price, Americans spent an estimated eight to twelve million dollars annually on daguerreotypes in the 1840s."

society and, in a few cases, the educated 'sons of nobodys.' This was a far cry from the Renaissance view, as expressed by Giovanni Paolo Lomazzo (1538-1600) in 1584, that 'only worthy, virtuous, or high-born individuals should be the subjects of portraits.'[264] The journeys undertaken by those Persians who had their portraits done in Europe and America were largely but not exclusively diplomatic in nature. One thing they all had in common, however, was their long duration. In a time when travel was slow and stays were long, ample opportunities arose for extra-curricular activities, like having one's portrait painted. The motivations behind the portraits varied. Sometimes an explicit reference explains why a particular portrait was commissioned or executed. In other cases we have no written record to help us understand why a portrait was done. Bearing in mind that, only in the case of Mar Yohanna, was the daguerreotype a coming medium that offered an alternative, albeit a relatively expensive one at first, to a miniature or full-sized portrait, it is not surprising that the European and American hosts of these Persian visitors wished their guests to be memorialized. Whatever the case may be, the record that these images provide is literally pricless. They put faces to names otherwise encountered in historical, diplomatic, military, political and religious literature of the time, and preserve images of Persians, some more eminent than others, from the Safavid through the early Qajar period, whose experiences outside of their home country undoubtedly left lasting impressions that never faded.

---

264. West 2004: 24-25. Cf. Pommier 1998 for the broader place of portraiture from the Renaissance through the Enlightenment.

BIBLIOGRAPHY

Anonymous. 1805. *Almanach du commerce de Paris, des Départemens de l'Empire français et des principales villes de l'Europe. An XIII.* Paris: Duverneuil and De la Tynna.

Anonymous. 1814. *Explication des ouvrages de peinture, sculpture, architecture et gravure, des artistes vivans, Exposés au Musée Royal des Arts, le 1.er Novembre 1814.* Paris: Dubray.

Anonymous. 1823. *The Boston Annual Advertiser annexed to the Boston Directory.* Boston: C. Stimpson, Jr. and J.H.A. Frost.

Anonymous. 1832. *Stimpson's Boston Directory; Containing the names of the inhabitants, their occupations, place of business, and dwelling houses, and the City Register, with lists of the streets, lanes and wharves, the city officers, public offices, and banks, and other useful information.* Boston: Stimpson and Clapp.

Anonymous. 1833. *Memoirs of American missionaries, formerly connected with the Society of Inquiry Respecting Missions, in the Andover Theological Seminary, embracing a history of the society, etc.* Boston: Pierce and Parker.

Anonymous. 1835. *Choicest works of Sir Thomas Lawrence.* London: Hodgson, Boys & Graves.

Anonymous. 1837. *First Exhibition and Fair of the Massachusetts Charitable Mechanic Association, at Faneuil and Quincy Halls, in the City of Boston, September 18, 1837.* Boston: Dutton and Wentworth.

Anonymous. 1842. *Strawberry Hill, the renowned seat of Horace Walpole, Mr. George Robins is honoured by having been selected by the Earl of Waldegrave, to sell by public competition, the Valuable Contents of Strawberry Hill…* Strawberry Hill.

Anonymous. 1845. *Peck's tourist's companion to Niagara Falls, Saratoga Springs, The Lakes, Canada, etc.* Buffalo NY: William B. & Charles E. Peck.

Anonymous. 1848. *The Nestorians of Persia: A history of the origin and progress of that People, and of missionary labours among them. With an account of the Nestorian massacres by the Koords. Written for the American Sunday-School*

Union, and revised by the Committee of Publication. Philadelphia: American Sunday-School Union.

Anonymous. 1850. *The Directory of the City of Boston: Embracing the city record, a general directory of the citizens, and a special directory of trades, professions, &c. with an almanac from July 1850, to July 1851.* Boston: George Adams.

Anonymous. 1852. *The Boston Directory, for the year 1852, embracing the city record, a general directory of the citizens, and a business directory, with an Almanac, from July, 1852, to July, 1853.* Boston: George Adams.

Anonymous. 1855. *The Directory of the City of Boston: Embracing the city record, a general directory of the citizens, and a business directory.* Boston: George Adams.

Anonymous. 1859. *Boston Directory, for the Year ending June 30, 1860, embracing the city record, a general directory of the citizens, and a business directory.* Boston: Adams, Sampson, and Co.

Anonymous. 1862. *A memorial of the semi-centennial celebration of the founding of Hamilton College, Clinton, N.Y.* Utica NY: Ellis H. Roberts.

Anonymous. 1866a. *Catalogue of the First Special Exhibition of National Portraits ending with the reign of King James the Second on loan to the South Kensington Museum, April 1866.* London: Strangeways and Walden.

Anonymous. 1866b. *The Boston Directory, for the year 1865, embracing the city record, a general directory of the citizens, and a business directory, for the year commencing July 1, 1866.* Boston: Sampson, Davenport, & Company.

Anonymous. 1882. Une grande imprimerie. *Bulletin de l'Imprimerie* 7 (January): 136.

Anonymous. 1889. Aus den Wanderjahren dreier estländischer Maler I. *Baltische Monatsschrift* 36: 708–747.

Anonymous. 1890a Aus den Wanderjahren dreier estländischer Maler II. *Baltische Monatsschrift* 37: 30–49.

Anonymous. 1890b. Aus den Wanderjahren dreier estländischer Maler III. *Baltische Monatsschrift* 37: 107–130.

Anonymous. 1896. *Special consular reports. Money and prices in foreign countries*, vol. 13/1. Washington DC: Government Printing Office.

Anonymous. 1899. *A catalogue of the literature and history of the British Islands, Part 1…* London: Bernard Quaritch.

Anonymous. 1908. *General catalogue of the Theological Seminary, Andover, Massachusetts, 1808–1908.* Boston: Thomas Todd.

Anonymous. 1911. *Inventaire général des dessins du Musée du Louvre…* Paris: Musée du Louvre.

Anonymous. 1913. Silhouettes rescued from the sea. *The Literary Digest* 47/19 (8 November): 874–875.

Anonymous. 1952. *Kellogg Prints: An Exhibition of the Work of J.G., D.W., E.B. and E.C. Kellogg; Hartford Lithographers 1830–1866, predecessors of Kellogg and Bulkeley.* Hartford CT: Connecticut Historical Society.

Anonymous. 1974. *Delacroix and the French Romantic print: An exhibition from the collection of Edwin Binney, 3rd.* Washington DC: Smithsonian Institution.

Anonymous. 2012. *248 portraits des 'invités' du Chancelier Metternich et de son épouse la Princesse Mélanie (vente aux enchères publiques.* Paris: Beaussant Lefèvre.

Ainsworth, W.F. 1841. An Account of a Visit to the Chaldeans, inhabiting Central Kurdistan; and of an Ascent of the Peak of Rowándiz (Ṭúr Sheïkíwá) in the Summer of 1840. *Journal of the Royal Geographical Society* 11: 21–76.

Amini, I. 1999. *Napoleon and Persia: Franco-Persian relations under the First Empire.* Washington DC: Mage Publishers.

Anderson, R.D. 1862. *Memorial volume of the first fifty years of the American Board of Commissioners for Foreign Missions*, 5th ed. Boston: Published by the Board.

Anderson, R.D. 1872. *History of the missions of the American Board of Commissioners for Foreign Missions to the Oriental Churches*, vol. 2. Boston: Congregational Publishing Society.

Andrea, B. 2017. *The lives of girls and women from the Islamic world in Early Modern British literature and culture.* Toronto/Buffalo/London: Univ. of Toronto Press.

Arasa, Y. 2019. *Davidiennes. Les femmes peintres de l'atelier de Jacques-Louis David (1768–1825).* Paris: L'Harmattan.

Armstrong, W.M. 1962. The many-sided world of Sir Robert Ker Porter. *The Historian* 25: 36–58.

Aronson, J. and Wieseman, M.E. 2006. *Perfect Likeness: European and American portrait miniatures from the Cincinnati Art Museum.* New Haven/London: Yale University Press.

Atai, F. 1992. *The sending of Iranian students to Europe, 1811–1906.* Unpubl. PhD diss., University of California, Berkeley.

Atkin, M. 1980. *Russia and Iran, 1780–1828.* Minneapolis: University of Minnesota Press.

Atkins, G. 2019. *Converting Britannia: Evangelicals and British public life, 1770–1840.* Woodbridge: The Boydell Press.

B., F. 1921. review of *Ancestors in silhouette cut by Auguste Edouart.. The Burlington Magazine for Connoisseurs* 39 (August): 92–93

Badger, G.P. 1852. *The Nestorians and their rituals: with the narrative of a mission to Mesopotamia and Coordistan in 1842–1844, and of a late visit to those countries in 1850; also, researches into the present condition of the Syrian Jacobites, Papal Syrians, and Chaldeans, and an inquiry into the religious tenets of the Yezeedees*, vol. 1. London: Joseph Masters.

Bally, J.T.H. 1907. *Francesco Bartolozzi, R.A. A biographical essay.* London: Otto Limited.

Barnett, R.D. 1972. Sir Robert Ker Porter: Regency artist and traveller. *Iran* 10: 19-24.

Beaussant, É. and Lefèvre, P.-Y. 2012. *Dessins et tableaux, objets d'art et de bel ameublement, tapis, vente aux enchères publiques, la mercredi 7 mars 2012 à 14 heures.* Paris: Beaussant Lefèvre.

Béland, M. 1992. *Painting in Quebec, 1820–1850: New views, new perspectives.* Québec City: Musée du Québec.

Bellier de la Chavignerie, E. and Auvray, L. 1882. *Dictionnaire général des Artistes de l'École française depuis l'origine des arts du dessin jusqu'à nos jours,* vol. 1. Paris: Librairie Renouard.

Bergmann, J. 1844. 213. Peter Fendi. *Neuer Nekrolog der Deutschen* 20/1: 619–626.

Blakesley, R.P. 2010. Pride and the politics of nationality in Russia's Imperial Academy of Fine Arts, 1757–1807. *Art History* 35/5: 800–835.

Bolton, E.S. 1915. *Wax portraits and silhouettes,* 2nd ed. Boston: The Massachusetts Society of the Colonial Dames of America.

Boon, K.G. 1992. *The Netherlandish and German drawings of the XVth and XVIth centuries of the Frits Lugt Collection,* vol. 1. Paris: Fondation Custodia.

Bouchot, H. 1910. *La Miniature française, 1750–1825.* Paris: Émile-Paul.

Bournoutian, G.A. 2014. *From Tabriz to St. Petersburg: Iran's mission of apology to Russia in 1829.* Costa Mesa CA: Mazda Publishers.

Bradford, S.H. 1869. *Scenes in the life of Harriet Tubman.* Auburn NY: W.J. Moses.

Brashears, C.C. 2009. Brief Biographies of the Kelloggs. P. 120 in Finlay, N., ed. *Picturing Victorian America: Prints by the Kellogg Brothers of Hartford, Connecticut, 1830–1880.* Hartford CT: Connecticut Historical Society.

Brinton, S. 1906. *Bartolozzi and his pupils in England, with an abridged list of his more important prints in line and stipple.* London: Siegle, Hill & Co.

Brock, S. 1996. The 'Nestorian' Church: A lamentable misnomer. *Bulletin of the John Rylands Library* 78: 23-35.

Brun-Durand, J. 1900. *Dictionnaire biographique et biblio-iconographique de La Drôme,* vol. 1. Grenoble: Librairie Dauphinoise.

Busch, N. 1902. *Geschichte der literärisch-praktischen Bürgerverbindung in Riga. 1802–1902. Spezieller Teil: Die Anstalten der Bürgerverbindung. I: Die Schulen.* Riga: W.F. Häcker.

Busse, H. 1972. *History of Persia under Qājār Rule, translated from the Persian of Ḥasan-e Fasā'i's Fārsnāma-ye Naṣeri.* New York/London: Columbia University Press.

Carey, J.T. 1954. *The American lithograph from its inception to 1865 with biographical considerations of twenty lithographers and a check list of their works.* Unpubl. PhD diss., The Ohio State University.

Carter, F. 1918. *An address delivered at the one hundredth anniversary of the founding of the Andover Theological Seminary, Tuesday, June 9, 1908.* Williamstown MA [no publisher given].

Castellucio, S. 2006. La Galerie des Glaces. Les réceptions d'ambassadeurs. *Versalia* 9: 37–44.

Chamberlain, M. 1908. *A documentary history of Chelsea including the Boston precincts of Winnisimmet, Rumney Marsh, and Pullen Point, 1624–1824*, vol. 2. Boston: The Massachusetts Historical Society.

Channing, E.W. 1921. *A history of the United States, Volume V. The period of transition, 1814–1848*. New York: The Macmillan Company.

Chenevière, A. 1916. Amélie Munier-Romilly, peintre, 1788–1875. *Nos anciens et leurs œuvres* 16: 105–160.

Cloake, M.M. 1988. *A Persian at the Court of King George, 1809–10: The journal of Mirza Abul Hassan Khan*. London: Barrie & Jenkins.

Costello, D.P. 1967. Griboedov as a diplomat. *Indiana Slavic Studies* 4: 52–73.

Coupin de la Couperie, M.–P. 1829. *Œuvres posthumes de Girodet-Trioson, peintre d'histoire; suivies de sa correspondance; précédées d'une notice historique, et mises en ordre*, vol. 1. Paris: Jules Renouard.

Crawford, M.C. 1915. *Social life in Old New England*. Boston: Little, Brown, and Company.

Crosby, D. 1843. Mar Yohannan and his people. Pp. 296–303 in Shepard, I.F., ed. *The Christian Souvenir: An offering for Christmas and the New Year*. Boston: Henry B. Williams.

Dagorne, R. 2005. Introduction. Pp. 12–15 in Dagorne, R., ed. *Au-delà du maître: Girodet et l'atelier de David*. Paris: Somogy.

Day, E.W. 1895. *One thousand years of Hubbard history, 866 to 1895: From Hubba, the Norse sea king to the enlightened present*. New York: Harlan Page Hubbard.

Delécluze, E.J. 1860. *Louis David, son école & son temps, souvenirs*, 2nd ed. Paris: Didier et Cie.

Deluga, W. 2008. The Oriental portraits of Aegidius Sadeler. *Print Quarterly* 25/4: 424–426.

Dexter, F.B. 1913. *Biographical notices of graduates of Yale College…* New Haven CT: Yale College.

Diba, L.S. 1989. Persian painting in the eighteenth century: Tradition and transmission. *Muqarnas* 6: 147–60.

Diba, L.S. 2011. Clothing x. In the Safavid and Qajar periods. *Encyclopaedia Iranica* (https://iranicaonline.org/articles/clothing-x accessed on 21 March 2021).

Diba, L.S. and Ekhtiar, M. 1999. *Royal Persian Paintings: The Qajar Epoch, 1785–1925*. London: I.B. Tauris.

Dickinson, S.N. 1841. *The Boston Almanac for the Year 1841*. Boston: Thomas Groom.

Dickinson, S.N. 1844. *The Boston Almanac for the Year 1844*. Boston: Thomas Groom.

Dickinson, S.N. 1847. *The Boston Almanac for the Year 1847*. Boston: Thomas Groom.

Dunlap, W. 1834. *History of the rise and progress of the arts of design in the United States*. New York: G.P. Scott and Co.

Duval, P.S. 1871. Lithography. Pp. 276-286 in Ringwalt, J.L., ed. *Encyclopædia of printing*. Philadelphia: Menamin & Ringwalt.

Dwight, B.W. 1871. *The history of the descendants of Elder John Strong, of Northampton, Mass.* Albany NY: Joel Munsell.

Eden, E. 1844. *Portraits of the princes and people of India*. London: J. Dickinson & Son.

Edouart, A. 1835. *A treatise on silhouette likenesses*. London: Longman and Company.

Edwards, J. and Burnage, S. 2017. *The British school of sculpture, c. 1760–1832*. Abingdon/New York: Routledge.

Ekbal, K. 1987. Die Brasilienreise des persischen Gesandten Mirza Abū'l-Ḥasan Khan Šīrāzī im Jahre 1810. *Die Welt des Islams* NS 27: 23–44.

Elliott, K. 2012. *Portraiture and British Gothic fiction: The rise of picture identification, 1764-1835*. Baltimore MD: The Johns Hopkins University Press.

Engelmann, G. 1840. *Traité théorique et pratique de lithographie*. Mulhouse: P. Baret.

English, C. 1995. *Nikolai Vasilyevich Gogol, Petersburg Tales, Marriage, The Government Inspector*. Oxford: Oxford University Press.

Evans, H. 1973. *John Kay of Edinburgh: Barber, miniaturist and social commentator, 1742–1826*. Aberdeen: Impulse Publications.

Fabian, M.H. 1983. *Mr. Sully, portrait painter: The works of Thomas Sully (1783–1872)*. Washington DC: National Portrait Gallery.

Falk, P.H. 1988. *The Annual Exhibition record of the Pennsylvania Academy of the Fine Arts, 1807–1870*. Madison CT: Sound View Press.

Ferrier, R.W. 1989. *The Arts of Persia*. New Haven/London: Yale University Press.

Fine, A. 1983. Césarine Davin-Mirvault: 'Portrait of Bruni' and other works by a student of David. *Woman's Art Journal* 4 (Spring-Summer): 15–20.

Floor, W. 1999a. Art (*naqqashi*) and artists (*naqqashan*) in Qajar Persia. *Muqarnas* 16: 125–154.

Floor, W. 1999b. *The Persian textile industry in historical perspective, 1500-1925*. Paris: Moyen Orient & Océan Indien XVIe-XIXe 11.

Fowler, W.C. 1858. *The English language in its elements and forms…* New York: Harper & Brothers.

Fraser, J.B. 1840. *Travels in Koordistan, Mesopotamia, &c. Including an account of parts of those countries hitherto unvisited by Europeans. With sketches of the character and manners of the Koordish and Arab tribe*s, vol. 1. London: Richard Bentley.

Gagel, D.V.S. 1998. *Ohio photographers: 1839–1900.* Nevada City NV: Carl Mautz Publishing.

Garstang, D. 1984. *Colnaghi, established 1760. Art, commerce, scholarship: A window onto the art world — Colnaghi 1760 to 1984.* London: P. & D. Colnaghi.

Gauzente, C. and Pascaud, B. 2018. À propos de la manière noire lithographique. Éléments techniques et retours d'expérience. *Nouvelles de l'estampe* 261: 108–119.

Gillespie, K. 2016. *The Early American daguerreotype: Cross-currents in art and technology.* Cambridge MA: MIT Press.

Goethe, J.W. 1867. *Goethes ausgewählte Werke,* vol. 14. Stuttgart: Verlag der J.G. Cotta'schen Buchhandlung.

Goetz, H. 1938. Persians and Persian costumes in Dutch painting of the seventeenth century. *The Art Bulletin* 20/3: 280–290.

Gombrich, E.H. 1969. *Art and illusion: A study in the psychology of pictorial representation.* Princeton: Princeton University Press.

Graves, A. 1905. *The Royal Academy of Arts: A complete dictionary of contributors and their work from its foundation in 1769 to 1904,* vol. 1. London: Henry Graves and Co. Ltd. and George Bell and Sons.

Green, N. 2014. *Terrains of exchange: Religious economies of global Islam.* Oxford: Oxford University Press.

Green, N. 2016. *The love of strangers: What six Muslim students learned in Jane Austen's London.* Princeton: Princeton University Press.

Greene, D. 1843. *Ministerial fidelity exemplified: A sermon at the funeral of the Rev. Daniel Crosby, late pastor of the Winthrop Church, Charlestown, March 3, 1843.* Boston: T.R. Marvin.

Groce, G.C. and Wallace, D.H. 1957. *The New-York Historical Society's Dictionary of Artists in America, 1564–1860.* New Haven: Yale University Press.

Groseclose, B. 1995. *British sculpture and the Company Raj: Church monuments and public statuary in Madras, Calcutta, and Bombay to 1858.* Newark DL: University of Delaware Press and London: Associated University Presses.

Groschwitz, G. von. 1954. The significance of XIX century color lithography. *Gazette des Beaux–arts* 6th ser. 44 (November): 243–266.

Grünstein, L. 1923. *Moritz Michael Daffinger und sein Kreis.* Vienna/Leipzig: Manz-Verlag.

Guthman, W.H. 1982. American militia drums, 1775–1845. *The Magazine Antiques* 122/1 (July): 148–155.

Hall, C. 1981. *Victorian illustrated music sheets.* London: Victoria & Albert Museum.

Hall, H. 1869. *The history of Auburn.* Auburn NY: Dennis Bro's & Co.

Hall, J. 2018. *Illustrated dictionary of symbols in Eastern and Western art.* New York/London: Routledge.

Halliday, T. 1999. *Facing the public: Portraiture in the aftermath of the French Revolution*. Manchester/New York: Manchester University Press.

Harden, E.J. 1979. *The murder of Griboedov: New materials*. Birmingham UK: Birmingham Slavonic Monographs 6.

Hare, R. 1965. *The art and artists of Russia*. London: Methuen.

Hart, C.H. 1900. The last of the silhouettists. *The Outlook* 66 (October 6): 329–335.

Herbette, M. 1907. *Une ambassade persane sous Louis XIV (d'après des documents inédits)*. Paris: Librairie académique Perrin et Cie.

Hippius, G.A. 1842. *Grundlinien einer Theorie der Zeichenkunst als Zweiges allgemeiner Schulbildung, nebst praktischer Anleitung für Lehrer und Lehrerinnen*. Leipzig: Rud. Hartmann.

Höflechner, W. and Wagner, A. 2011. *Joseph von Hammer–Purgtall: Briefe, Erinnerungen, Materialien*, vol. 2. Graz: Institut für Geschichte.

Holme, C. and Kennedy, H.A. 1917. *Early English portrait miniatures in the collection of the Duke of Buccleuch*. London/Paris/New York: 'The Studio' Ltd.

Hooker, E.W. 1839. *Memoir of Mrs. Sarah Lanman Smith*. Boston: Perkins & Marvin.

Howarth, D. 1997. *Images of rule: Art and politics in the English Renaissance, 1485–1649*. Berkeley/Los Angeles: University of California Press.

Idesbald, [?]. 1833. Relation historique de l'ambassade du Prince Khosrev-Mirza à Saint-Pétersbourg en 1829. *Revue de Paris* 14: 76–92.

Ikeda, A. 2019a. Cultural negotiation in early Sikh imagery: Portraiture of the Sikh Gurus to 1849. S*ikh Research Journal* 4/1: 21–44.

Ikeda, A. 2019b. The European influence on Sikh Portraiture: Representations of Maharaja Ranjit Singh, Sher-e-Punjab (the Lion of the Punjab). *The Chitrolekha Journal on Art and Design* 3: 1–16.

Jaubert, P.A. 1821. *Voyage en Arménie et en Perse, fait dans les années 1805 et 1806*. Paris: Chez Pélicier et Nepveu.

Johnston, H.M. 1998. *Ottoman and Persian odysseys: James Morier, creator of Hajji Baba of Ispahan, and his brothers*. London/New York: I.B. Tauris.

Karel, D. 1992. *Dictionnaire des artistes de langue française en Amérique du nord. Peintres, sculpteurs, dessinateurs, graveurs, photographes et orfèvres*: Québec City: Musée du Québec and Les Presses de l'Université de Laval.

Kaufmann, T.DaC. 1988. *The School of Prague: Painting at the Court of Rudolf II*. Chicago: University of Chicago Press.

Kayat, Y. 1839. *Journal of a Residence in England, and of a Journey from and to Syria, of their Royal Highnesses Reeza Koolee Meerza, Najaf Koolee Meerza, and Taymoor Meerza, of Persia*, vol. 1. London: printed for private circulation.

Kelly, L. 2006. *Diplomacy and murder in Tehran: Alexander Griboyedov and Imperial Russia's mission to the Shah of Persia*. London/New York: Tauris Parke Paperbacks.

Kerbs, D., Lebede, G. and Severin, G. 1976. *Historische Kunstpädagogik: Quellenlage, Forschungstand, Dokumentation*. Cologne: DuMont.

Ker Porter, R. 1821. *Travels in Georgia, Persia, Armenia, Ancient Babylonia, &c. &c. during the years 1817, 1818, 1819, and 1820*, vol. 1. London: Longman, Hurst, Rees, Orme, and Brown.

Knipe, P. 2002. Paper profiles: American portrait silhouettes. *Journal of the American Institute for Conservation* 41/3: 203–223.

Koschatzky, W. 1995. *Peter Fendi (1796–1842): Künstler, Lehrer und Leitbild*. Salzburg/Vienna: Residenz Verlag.

Koshoridze, I., Dgebuadze, M. and Beradze, G. 2013. New artistic trends and the portrait problem in the 19th century Iranian miniature painting. *Bulletin of the Georgian National Museum* 4 (49–B): 432–461 (in Georgian with English summary).

Krause, H.H. 2007. *Geschichte der Lithographie: Spiegelwelt — gespiegelte Welt*. Mannheim: Welz, Vermittler-Verlag.

Kuznetsova, I.A. 1980. *French painting from the Pushkin Museum: 17th to 20th century.* Moscow: Pushkin Museum.

Lane, W.C. and Browne, N.E. 1906. *A.L.A. Portrait Index: Index to portraits contained in printed books and periodicals*, vol. 3. Washington DC: Government Printing Office.

Lang, D.M. 1948. Griboedov's last years in Persia. *The American Slavic and East European Review* 7: 317–339.

Laurie, T. 1864. *Historical sketch of the Syria Mission*. New York: American Board of Commissioners for Foreign Missions.

Lazzeri, D., Nicoli, F. and Zhang, Y.X. 2019. Secret hand gestures in paintings. *Acta Biomedica* 90/4: 526-532.

Leatherwax, S.J. 2012. Peter S. Duval, Philadelphia's leading lithographer. Pp. 97–117 in Piola, E., ed. *Philadelphia on stone: Commercial lithography in Philadelphia, 1828–1878*. College Park PA: Penn State University Press.

Leavy, M.R. 1992. Looking for the Armenians: Eli Smith's missionary adventure, 1830–1831. *Transactions of the Connecticut Academy of Arts* 50 (December): 189–275.

Lécosse, C. 2013. Devenir peintre en miniature: la professionalisation des formations à la fin du XVIIIe siècle et au début du XIXe siècle. Pp. 97–114 in Bonnet, A. and Nerlich, F., eds. *Apprendre à peindre: Les ateliers privés à Paris, 1780–1863*. Paris: Presses Universitaires François-Rabelais.

Le Donne, J.P. 1987. Ruling families in the Russian political order, 1689–1825. *Cahiers du monde russe et soviétique* 28/3–4: 233–322.

Leek, P. 1999. *Russian painting: From the XVIIIth until the XXth century*. New York: Parkstone International.

Levey, M. 2005. *Sir Thomas Lawrence*. New Haven CT/London: Yale University Press.

Lienhard, H. 1898. *Californien unmittelbar vor und nach der Entdeckung des Goldes. Bilder aus dem Leben des Heinrich Lienhard von Bilten, Kanton Glarus in Nauvoo, Nordamerika. Ein Beitrag zur Jubiläumsfeier der Goldentdeckung und zur Kulturgeschichte Californiens*. Zürich: Fäsi & Beer.

Limouze, D. 1989. Aegidius Sadeler, Imperial Printmaker. *Philadelphia Museum of Art Bulletin* 85 (Spring): 1–24.

Longmate, B. 1810. *Stockdale's Peerage of England, Scotland and Ireland; Containing an account of all the Peers of the United Kingdom*, vol. 2. London: John Stockdale.

Lorenz, S. 2010. Pas à pas, lieux de mémoire des femmes à Genève. Pp. 55–65 in Koop, M.–C., ed. *La Francophonie en Europe: le cas de la Suisse romande et de la Communauté française de Belgique*. Brussels: Dialogues et Cultures 56.

Lowndes, W. 1870. Description of places on the banks of the River Thames, given during an excursion from Bourne End to Magna Charta Island. *Records of Buckinghamshire, or Papers and Notes on the History, Antiquities and Architecture of the County* 4: 395–420.

Mackenzie, G.N. 1917. *Colonial families of the United States of America…*, vol. 6. Baltimore MD: The Seaforth Press.

Maguire, R.A. 1995. *Exploring Gogol*. Palo Alto CA: Stanford University Press.

Marshall, L.A. 1957. Samuel Marsden Brookes. *California Historical Society Quarterly* 36: 193–203.

Marx, R. 1897. *Les médailleurs français depuis 1789. Notice historique suivie de documents sur la glyptique au dix-neuvième siècle*. Paris: Société de Propagation des Livres d'Art.

Matzer, U. 2015. 'Le modèle tout complet' — Vienna's Graphische Lehr- und Versuchsanstalt as a study center for visual communication. Pp. 28–56 in Gröning, M., ed. *Frame and focus: Photography as a schooling issue*. Vienna: Photographic Collection of the Albertina.

McPhee, C.C. and Orenstein, N.M. 2011. *Infinite jest: Caricature and satire from Leonardo to Levine*. New York: The Metropolitan Museum of Art.

Melville, F. 2013. Khosrow Mirza's mission to St Petersburg in 1829. Pp. 69–94 in Cronin, S., ed. *Iranian-Russian encounters: Empires and revolutions since 1800*. Abingdon/New York: Routledge.

Mercey, F. 1852. La gravure des médailles en France. *Revue des Deux Mondes* 14: 401–433.

Metternich, R. de. 1884. *Mémoires et écrits divers laissés par le Prince de Metternich, Chancelier de Cour et d'État*, vol. 8. Paris: Librairie Plon.

Millard, C.W. 1967. A diplomatic portrait: Lawrence's 'The Persian Ambassador.' *Apollo* 85 (February): 115–121.

Mohseni, S. and Andrews, P. 1992/2011. Clothing xvi. Kurdish clothing in Persia. *Encyclopaedia Iranica* (https://iranicaonline.org/articles/clothing-xvi accessed on 24 March 2021)

Mokhberi, S.M. 2020. *The Persian mirror: French reflections of the Safavid empire in Early Modern France.* New York: Oxford University Press.

Molyneux, N.Z.R. 1904. *History genealogical and biographical of the Molyneux Families.* Syracuse NY: C.W. Bardeen.

Montbel, G. de. 1832. *Le duc de Reichstadt.* Paris/Versailles: Le Normant and Angé.

Moreau, A. 1873. *E. Delacroix et son œuvre.* Paris: Librairie des Bibliophiles.

Morgan, D. 1998. *Visual piety: A history and theory of popular religious images.* Berkeley/Los Angeles/London: University of California Press.

Morier, J.J. 1812. *A journey through Persia, Armenia, and Asia Minor, to Constantinople, in the years 1808 and 1809…* London: Longman, Hurst, Rees, Orme, and Brown.

Motte, C. 1831. Lithographie à la manière noire. *L'Artiste* 1/2: 238-239.

Müller, H.A. and Singer, H.W. 1896. *Allgemeines Künstler-Lexicon*, vol. 2/1. Frankfurt: Rütten & Loening.

Müller-Simonis, P. 1892. *Du Caucase au Golfe persique à travers l'Arménie, le Kurdistan et la Mésopotamie.* Washington DC: Université Catholique d'Amérique.

Munsell, F. 1899. *American Ancestry: Giving the name and descent, in the male line, of Americans whose ancestors settled in the United States previous to the Declaration of Independence, A. D. 1776*, vol. 12. Albany NY: Joel Munsell's Sons.

Nagler, G.K. 1835. *Neues algemeines Künstler-Lexicon; oder Nachrichten von dem Leben und den Werken der Maler, Bildhauer, Baumeister, Kupferstecher etc.*, vol. 1. Munich: E.A. Fleischmann.

Néret, G. 2000. *Eugène Delacroix, 1798–1863: The prince of Romanticism.* Cologne/London/Los Angeles/Madrid/Paris/Tokyo: Taschen.

Nevill Jackson, E. 1911. *The history of silhouettes.* London: The Connoisseur.

Nevill Jackson, E. 1921. *Ancestors in silhouette cut by Auguste Edouart. Illustrative notes and biographical sketches by Mrs. F. Nevill Jackson.* London/New York: John Lane Co.

Nevill Jackson, E. n.d. *Catalogue of 3,800 Named and Dated American Silhouette Portraits by August Edouart, 1789–1861…discovered by Mrs. E. Nevill Jackson…* London [no publisher given].

Nylander, J.C. 1994. *Our own snug fireside: Images of the New England home, 1760–1860.* New York: Alfred A. Knopf.

O'Brien, D.C. 2003. The early nineteeth-century Boston engraving trade, and the engravers who developed it. *Printing History* 45: 3–17.

Oliver, A. 1970. *Portraits of John Quincy Adams and his wife.* Cambridge MA: The Belknap Press of Harvard University Press.

Oliver, A. 1977. *Auguste Edouart's silhouettes of eminent Americans, 1839-1844.* Washington DC: National Portrait Gallery, Smithsonian Institution.

Oliver, L. 2006. Christoffer Wilhelm Eckersberg (1783–1853), portrait of Bertel Thorvaldsen 1838. P. 52 in Sturgis, A., Christiansen, R., Oliver, L. and Wilson, M., eds. *Rebels and Martyrs: The Image of the Artist in the Nineteenth Century.* London: National Gallery Company Limited.

Olivier, G.-A. 1808. *Reise durch Persien und Klein–Asien.* Leipzig: J.C. Hinrichs.

O'Malley, T. 2014. 'Plants in their perfection': The Botanical Garden and the illustrated book. Pp. 53–78 in Fraser, S.M. and Sellers, V.B., eds. *Flora Illustrata: Great works from the LuEsther T. Mertz Library of the New York Botanical Garden.* New Haven/London: Yale University Press.

Packard, T. 1854. *A history of the churches and ministers, and of Franklin Association in Franklin County, Mass.* Boston: S.K. Whipple and Company.

Parker, A.L. and Kaplan, M. 1959. *Charles Fenderich: Lithographer of American statesmen.* Washington DC: Library of Congress.

Paton, H. 1838. *A series of original portraits and caricature etchings by the late John Kay, Miniature painter, Edinburgh; with biographical sketches and illustrative anecdotes*, vol. 2/2. Edinburgh: Hugh Paton.

Paucker, J. 1848. *Die Literatur der Geschichte Liv-, Ehst- und Curlands aus den Jahren 1836 bis 1847 in übersichtlicher Zusammenstellung.* Dorpat: Druck und Verlag von Laakmann.

Payer von Thurn, R. 1907. Mirza Abul Hassan Chan. *Chronik des Wiener Goethe-Vereins* 21: 18–24.

Pennell, J. and Pennell, E. 1898. *Lithography & Lithographers: Some chapters in the history of the art.* New York: The Century Co. and London: T. Fisher Unwin.

Perkins, H.M. 1887. *Life of Justin Perkins, D.D. Pioneer missionary to Persia.* Chicago: Woman's Presbyterian Board of Missions of the Northwest.

Perkins, J. 1861. *A Residence of eight years in Persia and missionary life in Persia: Being glimpses at a quarter of a century of labors among the Nestorian Christians.* Boston: American Tract Society.

Petrova, Y.A. 2004. *Roads in Russian art at the State Russian Museum.* St. Petersburg: Palace Editions.

Pierce, S. and Slautterback, C. 1991. *Boston lithography, 1825–1880: The Boston Athenaeum Collection.* Boston: Boston Athenaeum.

Polak, J.E. 1865. *Persien. Das Land und seine Bewohner. Ethnographische Schilderungen*, vol. 1. Leipzig: F.A. Brockhaus.

Pommier, É. 1998. *Théories du portrait. De la Renaissance aux Lumières.* Paris: Gallimard.

Potts, D.T. 2022. *Agreeable news from Persia: Iran in the Colonial and early Republican American press, 1712–1848*, 3 vols. Wiesbaden: Springer.

Potts, D.T. n.d. *A nook in the temple of fame: French officers in Persian service, 1808–1826.*

Prime, S.I. 1875. *The life of Samuel F.B. Morse, LL.D., inventor of the electromagnetic recording telegraph.* New York: D. Appleton and Company.

Prior, M.A. 2011. *An Indian portfolio: The life and work of Emily Eden.* London: Quartet Books.

Raby, J. 2001. *Qajar portraits: Figure paintings from nineteenth century Persia.* London: I.B. Tauris.

Relia, A. 2014. *The Indian portrait – III: A historical journey of graphic prints up to Independence.* Surat/Ahmedabad: Archer Art Gallery.

Reps, J.W. 1984. *Views and viewmakers of urban America: Lithographs of towns and cities in the United States and Canada, notes on the artists and publishers, and a Union Catalog of their work, 1825–1925.* Columbia MO: University of Missouri Press.

Reynolds, J. 1846. A memoir of the late Right Hon. Sir Gore Ouseley, Bart., sometime Ambassador Extraordinary and Plenipotentiary at the Court of Persia. Pp. v–ccxxvi in Ouseley, G. *Biographical notices of Persian poets…* London: The Oriental Translation Fund.

Rizvi, K. 2012. The suggestive portrait of Shah 'Abbas: Prayer and likeness in a Safavid *Shahnama. The Art Bulletin* 94/7: 226–50.

Robaut, A., Chesneau, E. and Calmettes, F. 1885. *L'œuvre complet de Eugène Delacroix: Peintures, dessins, gravures, lithographies.* Paris: Charavay Frères Èditeurs.

Robinson, B.W. 1963. The court painters of Fath Ali Shah. *Eretz-Israel* 7: 94–105.

Robinson, B.W. 1986. Art in Iran x.2 Qajar painting. *Encyclopædia Iranica* 2: 637–40.

Rondot, N. 1904. *Les médailleurs et les graveurs de monnaies, jetons et médailles en France.* Paris: Ernest Leroux.

Rosenthal, D. 1979. Joseph Franque's 'Scene during the Eruption of Vesuvius.' *Philadelphia Museum of Art Bulletin* 75 (March): 2–15.

Rovinsky, D.A. 1895. ГАМПЕЛЬН'Ъ, Карлъ (Hampeln). *Podrobnyĭ slovar'russkikh graverov XVI-XIX vv* [*A Detailed Dictionary of Russian Engravers of the XVIth-XIXth Centuries*] 1: 150–151.

Royle, J.F. 1839. *Illustrations of the botany and other branches of Natural History of the Himalayan Mountains, and of the flora of Cashmere*, vol. 2. London: W.H. Allen and Co.

Salamon, F. 1996. *Anmut des Nordens: Wilhelm Heuer und sein graphisches Werk.* Neumünster: Karl Wachholtz Verlag.

Schaechter, E. 1997. *In the company of mushrooms.* Cambridge MA: Harvard University Press.

Schell, S. 1923. The silhouette and how it got its name. *The Mentor* 11/9 (October): 39.

Schidlof, L.R. 1964. *The miniature in Europe in the 16th, 17th, 18th, and 19th centuries*, vol. 1. Graz: Akademische Druck– und Verlagsanstalt.

Schultes, L. 2002. 'Der arme Maler'. Zur sozialen Lage der Künstler im Wiener Biedermeier. *Studien zur Musikwissenschaft* 50: 59–80.

Schwartz, G. 2013. The Sherleys and the Shah: Persia as the stakes in a Rogue's Gambit. Pp. 78–99 in Langer, A., ed. *The Fascination of Persia: The Persian–European dialogue in seventeenth-century art & contemporary art from Tehran.* Zürich: Museum Rietberg.

Seaman, E.C. 1852. *Essays on the progress of nations, in civilization, productive industry, wealth and population.* New York: Charles Scribner.

Sevaistre, O. 1996. Missions françaises en Perse en 1805 et 1810. *Revue d'histoire diplomatique* 110/3–4: 191–200.

Seward, F.W. 1891. *William H. Seward: An autobiography from 1801 to 1834. With a memoir of his life, and selections from his letters, 1831-1846.* New York: Derby and Miller.

Simond, C. 1900. *Paris de 1800 à 1900 d'après les estampes et les mémoires du temps.* Paris: Librairie Plon.

Sjöberg, Y. 1963. *Pour comprendre Delacroix.* Paris: Beauchesne et ses fils.

Smith, E. 1833. *Researches of the Rev. E. Smith and Rev. H.G.O. Dwight in Armenia: including a journey through Asia Minor, and into Georgia and Persia, with a visit to the Nestorian and Chaldean Christians of Oormiah and Salmas*, 2 vols. Boston: Crocker and Brewster and New York: Jonathan Leavitt.

Soucek, P. 2000. The theory and practice of portraiture in the Persian tradition. *Muqarnas* 17: 97–108.

Spinicci, P. 2009. Portraits: Some phenomenological remarks. *Proceedings of the European Society for Aesthetics* 1: 37–59.

Staiti, P.J. 1981. Samuel F.B. Morse's search for a personal style: The anxiety of influence. *Winterthur Portfolio* 16/4 (Winter): 253–281.

Still, W. 1872. *The Underground Railroad. A record of facts, authentic narratives, letters, yc., narrating the hardships, hair-breadth escapes and death struggles of the slaves in their efforts for freedom, as relayed by themselves and others, or witnessed by the author.* Philadelphia: Porter & Coates.

Stites, R. 2005. *Serfdom, society, and the arts in Imperial Russia: The pleasure and the power.* New Haven CT/London: Yale University Press.

Stone, W.L. Jr. 1875. *Reminiscences of Saratoga and Ballston.* New York: Virtue & Yorston.

Thomson, T. 1875. *Biographical Dictionary of Eminent Scotsmen*, vol. 2. London: Blackie and Son.

Thwaites, R.G. 1889. *First Triennial Catalogue of the Portrait Gallery of the Historical Society of Wisconsin.* Madison WI: State Historical Society.

Thwaites, R.G. 1892. *Second Triennial Catalogue of the Portrait Gallery of the Historical Society of Wisconsin.* Madison WI: State Historical Society.

Todd, F.P. 1939. The Huddy & Duval prints: An adventure in military lithography. *The Journal of the American Military Institute* 3/3: 166–176.

Totten, J.R. 1916. Thacher-Thatcher Genealogy. *The New York Genealogical and Biographical Record* 47/3 (July): 257–280.

Tuer, A.W. 1885. *Bartolozzi and his works: A biographical & descriptive account of the life and career of Francesco Bartolozzi, R.A.* London: Field & Tuer.

Tuer, A.W. 1890. Edouart's silhouettes. *Notes and Queries* 7th ser. 10 (30 August): 170.

Vahdat, V. 2017. *Occidentalist perceptions of European architecture in nineteenth-century Persian travel diaries: Travels in Farangi space.* London/New York: Routledge.

Veillon, P. 1908. Munier-Romilly, Mme Amélie. *Schweizerisches Künstler-Lexikon* 2: 451.

Vernay, A.S. 1913. *American silhouette portraits cut by August Edouart: A notable collection of portraits taken between 1839–1849.* New York: Arthur S. Vernay.

Vernay, A.S. 1914. The cult of the silhouette illustrated by the work of Miers, Edouart and others. *The House Beautiful* 35/3: 82–85.

Vosoughi, J. 2016. The examination of Persian calligraphy in publications of Qajar period. *International Journal of Humanities and Cultural Studies* (January): 1263–1271.

Wairy, L.C. 1830. *Mémoires de Constant, premier valet de chambre de l'Empereur, sur la vie privée de Napoléon, sa famille et sa cour,* vol. 4. Paris: Chez Ladvocat.

Walker, A. 1852. *Beauty illustrated by an analysis and classification of beauty in woman, with a critical view of the hypotheses of Hume, Hogarth, Burke, Knight, Alison, etc. and of the hypotheses of beauty in sculpture and painting, by Leonardo da Vinci, Winckelmann, Mengs, Bossi, etc.* London: Henry G. Bohn.

Weckbecker, W. Freiherr von. 1902. *Handbuch der Kunstpflege in Österreich,* 3rd ed. Vienna: Im Kaiserlich-Königlichen Schulbücher-Verlage.

Weilbach, P. 1877–1878. *Nyt Dansk Kunstnerlexikon, indeholdende Korte Levnedstegnelser over Konstnere som indtil udgangen af 1876 have levet og arbejdet i Danmark eller den Danske Stat.* Copenhagen: Andr. Fred. Høst & Søns Forlag.

Weitenkampf, F. 1912. *American graphic art.* New York: Henry Holt and Company.

West, S. 2004. *Portraiture.* Oxford: Oxford University Press.

Westmacott, C.M. 1823. *A descriptive and critical catalogue to the Exhibition of the Royal Academy, The Fifty-fifth.* London: John Bairburn.

Wille, H. 2001. Botanical collectors and collections in the Low Countries. Pp. 77–95 in Vande Walle, W.F. and Kasaya, K., eds. *Dodonæus in Japan: Translation and the Scientific Mind in the Tokugawa Period*. Leuven: Leuven University Press and Kyoto: International Research Center for Japanese Studies.

Williams, D.E. 1831. *The life and correspondence of Sir Thomas Lawrence, Kt.*, vol. 2. London: Henry Colburn and Richard Bentley.

Woods-Marsden, J. 2008. Assessments. Pp. 360–365 in Elkins, J. and Williams, R., eds. *Renaissance Theory*. New York/London: Routledge.

Würtenberger, T. 2017. *Symbole der Freiheit: Zu den Wurzeln westlicher politischer Kultur*. Vienna/Cologne/Weimar: Böhlau Verlag.

Wurzbach, C. 1858. *Biographisches Lexikon des Kaiserthums Oesterreich*, vol. 4. Vienna: Druck und Verlag der typogr.-literar.-artist. Anstalt.

Wust, K.G. 1959. German immigrants and their newspapers in the District of Columbia. *Report of the Society for the History of Germans in Maryland* 30: 36–66.

Index

OTHER MAGE TITLES

History of Bread in Iran

Studies in the History of Medicine in Iran

Salar al-Dowleh: A Delusional Prince and Wannabe Shah

Kermanshah: City and Province, 1800-1945

History of Hospitals in Iran, 550–1950

The Beginnings of Modern Medicine in Iran

Food Security in Iran: Edareh-ye Arzaq, 1910–1935

ANNOTATED TRANSLATIONS

German Sources on Safavid Persia
Exotic Attractions in Persia, 1684–1688: Travels & Observations
Engelbert Kaempfer

A Man of Two Worlds: Pedros Bedik in Iran, 1670–1675
translated with Colette Ouahes from the Latin

Astrakhan Anno 1770
Samuel Gottlieb Gmelin

Travels Through Northern Persia 1770–1774
Samuel Gottlieb Gmelin

Titles and Emoluments in Safavid Iran: A Third Manual of Safavid
Administration
Mirza Naqi Nasiri

Persia: An Area Study, 1633
Joannes de Laet
translated with Colette Ouahes from the Latin

WILLEM FLOOR IN COLLABORATION WITH HASAN JAVADI
Persian Pleasures
How Iranians Relaxed Through the Centuries
with Food, Drink and Drugs

Awake: A Moslem Woman's Rare Memoir of Her Life
and Partnership with the Editor of Molla Nasreddin,
the Most Influential Satirical Journal of the Caucasus and Iran,
1907–1931

The Heavenly Rose-Garden: A History of Shirvan & Daghestan
Abbas Qoli Aqa Bakikhanov

Travels in Iran and the Caucasus, 1652 and 1655
Evliya Chelebi

POETRY

Faces of Love: Hafez and the Poets of Shiraz – Bilingual Edition
Translated by Dick Davis

The Mirror Of My Heart:
A Thousand Years of Persian Poetry by Women, Bilingual Edition
Translated by Dick Davis

Pearls That Soak My Dress: Elegies for a Child
Jahan Malek Khatun/ translated by Dick Davis

Layli and Majnun
Nezami Ganjavi / Translated by Dick Davis

Shahnameh: the Persian Book of Kings
Abolqasem Ferdowsi / Translated by Dick Davis

The Lion and the Throne

Fathers and Sons

Sunset of Empire

Rostam: Tales of Love and War from Persia's Book of Kings
Abolqasem Ferdowsi / Translated by Dick Davis

Borrowed Ware: Medieval Persian Epigrams
Introduced and Translated by Dick Davis

At Home and Far from Home
Poems on Iran and Persian Culture
Dick Davis

They Broke Down the Door: Poems
Fatemeh Shams / Introduction and translations by Dick Davis

The Layered Heart: Essays on Persian Poetry
In Celebration of Dick Davis
Edited by Ali-Asghar Seyyed Ghorab

Another Birth and Other Poems
By Forugh Farrokhzad, translated by Hasan Javadi and Susan Sallée
Bilingual edition

Obeyd-e Zakani: Ethics of Aristocrats and other Satirical Works
translated by Hasan Javadi

Milkvetch and Violets
Mohammad Reza Shafi'i-Kadkani/ translated by Mojdeh Bahar

Cookbooks by Najmieh Batmanglij

*Food of Life: Ancient Persian and
Modern Iranian Cooking and Ceremonies*

Joon: Persian Cooking Made Simple

Cooking in Iran: Regional Recipes and Kitchen Secrets

Silk Road Cooking: A Vegetarian Journey

From Persia to Napa: Wine at the Persian Table
With Dick Davis, Burke Owens

A Taste of Persia

Cinema

The Films of Makhmalbaf: Cinema, Politics, and Culture in Iran
Eric Egan

Masters & Masterpieces of Iranian Cinema
Hamid Dabashi

My Favorite Films
Cyrus Ghani

Persia Observed Series

*The Strangling of Persia:
A Story of European Diplomacy and Oriental Intrigue*
Morgan Shuster

The Persian Revolution of 1905-1909
Edward Brown / Introduction by Abbas Amanat

*In the Land of the Lion & Sun:
Experiences of Life in Persia from 1866-1881*
C. J. Wills / Introduction by Abbas Amanat

*A Man of Many Worlds:
The Diaries and Memoirs of Dr. Ghasem Ghani*
Ghasem Ghani / Edited by Cyrus Ghani

FICTION

My Uncle Napoleon
Iraj Pezeshkzad / Translated by Dick Davis

Savushun: A Novel about Modern Iran
Simin Daneshvar / Translated by M.R. Ghanoonparvar

Daneshvar's Playhouse: A Collection of Stories
Simin Daneshvar / Translated by Maryam Mafi

Sutra and Other Stories
Simin Daneshvar / Translated by Hasan Javadi & Amin Neshati

Stories from Iran: A Chicago Anthology 1921-1991
Edited by Heshmat Moayyad

Garden of the Brave in War
Terence O'Donnell

King of the Benighted
Houshang Golshiri / Translated by Abbas Milani

Black Parrot, Green Crow: A Collection of Short Fiction
Houshang Golshiri / Translated by Heshmat Moayyad et al.

Seven Shades of Memory: Stories of Old Iran
Terence O'Donnell

HISTORY & MEMOIR

The Persian Sphinx:
Amir Abbas Hoveyda and the Iranian Revolution
Abbas Milani

Discovering Cyrus: The Persian Conqueror
Astride the Ancient World
Reza Zarghamee

Tarikh-e Azodi, Life at the Court of the Early Qajar Shahs
Soltan Ahmad Mirza Azod al-Dowleh,
Edited and Translated Manoutchehr M. Eskandari-Qajar

The Artist and the Shah: Memoirs of Life at the Persian Court
Dust-Ali Khan "Mo`ayyer al-Mamalek,
Translated, Edited, Introduced, and annotated by
Manoutchehr M. Eskandari-Qajar

Crowning Anguish: Taj al-Saltaneh
Memoirs of a Persian Princess
Introduction by Abbas Amanat / Translated by Anna Vanzan

HISTORY & MEMOIR

Tales of Two Cities: A Persian Memoir
Abbas Milani

Lost Wisdom:
Rethinking Modernity in Iran
Abbas Milani

French Hats in Iran
Heydar Radjavi

Father Takes a Drink and Other Memories of Iran
Heydar Radjavi

The Persian Garden: Echoes of Paradise
Mehdi Khansari / M. R. Moghtader / Minouch Yavari

Closed Circuit History
Ardeshir Mohassess, foreword by Ramsey Clark

Mosaddegh: Ahead of Their Time, Book 1
Nicolas Gorjestani

Zviad: Ahead of Their Time, Book 2
Nicolas Gorjestani

A Scholar for Out Times:
A Celebration of the Life & Work of Shahrokh Meskoob
Abbas Milan & C. Ryan Perkins (eds.)

Audio Books

Faces of Love: Hafez and the Poets of Shiraz
Translated by Dick Davis / Penguin Audio / Read by
Dick Davis, Tala Ashe and Ramiz Monsef

The Mirror of My Heart:
A Thousand Years of Persian Poetry by Women
Translated by Dick Davis / Penguin Audio / Read by
Dick Davis, Mozhan Marno, Tala Ashe and Serena Manteghi

Layli and Majnun
Nezami Ganjavi / Translated by Dick Davis
Penguin Audio / Read by
Dick Davis, Peter Ganim, Serena Manteghi and Sean Rohani

Vis and Ramin
Fakhraddin Gorgani / Translated by Dick Davis
Mage Audio / Read by
Mary Sarah Agliotta, Dick Davis (introduction)

My Uncle Napoleon
Iraj Pezeshkzad / Translated by Dick Davis
Mage Audio / Read by
Moti Margolin, Dick Davis (introduction)

Savushun: A Novel about Modern Iran
Simin Daneshvar / Translated by M.R. Ghanoonparvar
Mage Audio / Read by
Mary Sarah Agliotta, Brian Spooner (introduction)

Crowning Anguish: Taj al-Saltaneh
Memoirs of a Persian Princess
from the Harem to Modernity, 1884–1914
Introduction by Abbas Amanat / Translated by Anna Vanzan
Mage Audio / Read by
Kathreen Khavari